OF HOCKEY
AND HIJAB

*Reflections of a Canadian
Muslim Woman*

Sheema Khan

We acknowledge the support of
the Canada Council for the Arts for our publishing program.

 Canada Council   Conseil des Arts
for the Arts   du Canada

 ONTARIO ARTS COUNCIL
CONSEIL DES ARTS DE L'ONTARIO

We also acknowledge support from
the Government of Ontario through the Ontario Arts Council.

Cover design: David Drummond, Salamander Hill Design

Library and Archives Canada Cataloguing in Publication

Khan, Sheema

Of hockey and hijab : reflections of a Canadian Muslim woman / Sheema
Khan.

ISBN 978-1-894770-56-9

1. Islam. 2. Women in Islam—Canada. I. Title.

BP161.3.K4365 2009   297   C2009-902520-5

Printed in Canada by Coach House Printing

TSAR Publications
P. O. Box 6996, Station A
Toronto, Ontario M5W 1X7
Canada

www.tsarbooks.com

CONTENTS

INTRODUCTION   *v*

THE HIGHJACKING OF ISLAM

Was He Not a Human Soul?   3
The Abuse of Islamic Language   5
Reforming Islam   8
The Virtuous Jihad   10
The Seduction of Terror: How to Counter It   13
Bin Laden vs The Prophet (1): A War of Ideas   17
Bin Laden vs The Prophet (2): Two Opposing Visions . . .   20
Acknowledging Fanaticism   23

LIVING IN FEAR: CANADIAN WHILE MUSLIM

Don't Shackle Us to 9/11   29
Canadian While Muslim   32
Living with Fear   35
Double Standards   37
Ugly Then, Ugly Now   40
It's Still Nasty Out There   44
Exposing Anti-Muslim Discomfort   47
Deliver Us from Suspicion   49
Canadian Double-talk   52
The Government's Discrimination   55
Outsourcing Torture: Government Duplicity   59

ISLAM IN THE WORLD

This Way Forward for Muslims   65
Why Muslims Are Angry   68
Love-Hate   71
Islamic Financing   74
Neighbourly Love and Mideast Debate   77

Islamic Democracy? 79

Fearing Dubai 83

Using the Lessons of Canada to Heal the Wounds ... 86

Funny 88

The Soul in Science 91

THE CANADIAN WAY

I Was a Teenage Hijabi Hockey Player 99

There Really Is a Canadian Way 101

Looking to the Charter 104

Facing New Identities 106

Make Room for the Spiritual in Educating Our Young 109

China's Hui and a Muslim Model for Canada 112

A Leader Who Knows How to Serve 114

Democracy, Peace, and Sharia Law 116

There's Nothing Like Watching the Montreal Canadiens ... 118

THE RIGHTS OF WOMEN

Putting Women First 125

Storming the Harvard Bastion 127

Sharia-phobia 130

Banning Hijab: the New Colonialism 134

No Veiled Threat 137

Hijabs: Don't Kick Up a Fuss 140

Our Right to Flash Some Veil 142

Don't Misread the Koran 145

Uprooting Age-old Customs from Within 147

The Koran Does Not Sanction Wife-beating 150

A Hero for Our Times 152

What Closed-minded Liberals Can Learn from ... 155

The Sorrow and the Pity of "Honour" 157

Acknowledgements 161

Introduction

In the fall of 2002, I was asked to write a monthly column for *The Globe and Mail*, Canada's national newspaper, on issues pertaining to Islam and Muslims, in view of the events of September 11, 2001. Up to that point, I had written a few op-ed pieces for *The Globe*, *The Toronto Star*, and the *Montreal Gazette* on some horrific events overseas. I was struck by the profound vision of Mariane Pearle in face of the murder of her husband Daniel Pearle, and revolted by the naked anti-Semitism of those who committed the depraved act. I was inspired by the indomitable courage of Mukhtar Mai in the face of her brutal tribal rape. As the Israeli-Palestinian conflict raged during the second intifada, I remembered the genuine love extended to me by my Jewish neighbours. The best of human actions in the face of disheartening acts. And so began this venture to write about Islam and Muslims for a Canadian audience, from a Canadian Muslim perspective.

These essays appeared as monthly columns in *The Globe and Mail* from 2002 to 2009, except for "Let Neighbourly Love," which appeared in the *Montreal Gazette*. My *Globe* editors, Patrick Martin and the late Val Ross, encouraged me to write on topics of my choosing. Often, the topics dealt with issues in the news, overseas and local. I tried to provide a nuanced perspective of events, which often elicited thoughtful feedback (along with a few instances of hate mail).

The article about the controversy over the Prophet Muhammad cartoons elicited the greatest response. In it, the stark difference between the irrational actions of some Muslims and the teachings of Prophet Muhammad were highlighted; this turned out to be an eye-opener for many readers.

In addition, *Globe* readers have provided much valuable feedback that has contributed to my own understanding of Islam, and an appreciation of the diversity of thought in this nation. It has been a privilege to have a national conversation about issues which are important to all Canadians.

Over the years, however, the focus has been primarily on domestic issues such as reasonable accommodation, religiously-based family arbitration, multiculturalism, "home-grown" terrorism, and the targeting of innocent Muslims by the security services. In short, the spotlight has been on two main features: the struggle between security and civil liberties; and the tension between integration and identity. The latter, I believe, is a dynamic that has not been fully explored. At its heart is a debate which has only begun—over the position of Muslim women within Muslim society, and within the larger Canadian society. In particular, there is a gaping chasm between the treatment of women within many Muslim cultures, and the central teachings of the Koran and the Prophetic example.

In the Jan/Feb 2007 issue of the American journal *Foreign Affairs*, Dominique Moïsi of the French Institute of International Relations wrote that contemporary world tensions were not symptomatic of a clash of civilizations, but rather a result of interdependent layers of conflict. One such layer is an emotional clash between cultures of fear and humiliation. Bridging this divide will require a culture of dialogue. Given the Canadian propensity to talk through— rather than fight over—issues of conflict, our strength lies in the belief that a culture of dialogue transcends these divides. Our common commitment to a culture of human dignity will eventually overcome these mutually antagonistic cultures of fear and humiliation. This should serve us well as we face the challenges of the 21st century.

Sheema Khan, Ottawa, October 2009

The Highjacking of Islam

Was He Not a Human Soul?

The brutal manner in which the American reporter Daniel Pearl was killed is horrific enough.[1] It was even more repulsive to know that Mr Pearl was kidnapped, murdered, and mutilated simply because he was a Jew. As a Muslim who has been involved in fighting discrimination and hate directed at Muslims over the past few years, I thought I knew how destructive hate could be. But Mr Pearl's murder in 2002 brought home a chilling reality.

That "Muslims," ostensibly "fighting" for the liberation of their oppressed brethren, seeking to "embarrass" Pakistani President Pervez Musharraf, would engage in such a barbaric act and murder a man simply because he was a Jew is an affront to Muslims everywhere, and is completely rejected by the very foundations of Islam. As for the bombing a few weeks earlier in Netanya, Israel—the murder of people who were engaged in worship, be it for Sunday service or Passover, is vile, and condemned in Islam. Muslims must denounce such acts in the strongest of terms.

Tariq Ramadan, a philosophy professor based in Switzerland, is one Muslim intellectual who has strongly criticized anti-Jewish sentiment among Muslims. Writing in *Le Monde*, he said: "Much like the situation across the Muslim world, there exists in France today a discourse which is anti-Semitic, seeking legitimacy in certain Islamic texts and support in the present situation in Palestine. This is the attitude of not only marginalized youth, but also of intellectuals and imams, who see the manipulative hand of the 'Jewish lobby' at each turn or every political setback . . . Nothing in

Islam can legitimize xenophobia or the rejection of a human being due to his/her religious creed or ethnicity. One must say unequivocally, with force, that anti-Semitism is unacceptable and indefensible. The message of Islam requires respect of Jewish faith and spirituality as noble expressions of 'The People of the Book.' "

He continues; "Muhammad constantly taught respect for all human beings, with all their differences. One day, he stood up out of respect when he heard a funeral procession nearby. When told it was that of a Jew, he answered: 'Was he not a human soul?' It is the shared responsibility of Muslim intellectuals to articulate a comprehensive Islamic message that emphasizes personal responsibility and respect for others."

Respect for others seems to be sorely lacking in parts of the Muslim world. Acts of terror and destruction by zealots is contemptible. Yet there is hope. In spite of her personal anguish, the words of Mr Pearl's pregnant widow, Mariane, were inspiring: "Revenge would be easy, but it is far more valuable in my opinion to address this problem of terrorism with enough honesty to question our own responsibility as nations and as individuals for the rise of terrorism . . . [I hope] I will be able to tell our son that his father carried the flag to end terrorism, raising an unprecedented demand among people from all countries not for revenge but for the values we all share: love, compassion, friendship and citizenship, far transcending the so-called clash of civilizations."

The universal values enunciated by Ms Pearl are richly entrenched in Islam. Muslims who live in the West are living proof that a society based on pluralism, social justice, and rule of law is not anathema to living the faith of Islam. Such social harmony was also successfully achieved during various periods of Islamic history.

We Muslims of the West have a duty to serve as examples to our co-religionists elsewhere. We must confront the binary vision of "us" versus "them" with the reality of a prosperous civil society based on respect for oneself and others. We must counter xenophobia with the truth that we have found human kindness in our neighbours, friends, and co-workers of diverse backgrounds.

At the same time, we have a duty to educate our neighbours about ongoing injustices that need to be addressed in Kashmir, Palestine, and Chechnya. Legitimate criticism of Israel should not be confused with anti-Semitism, nor should it be construed as criticism of Judaism. The common monotheistic foundation of Islam and Judaism is far stronger than the forces that seek to sow mistrust between the two communities, both of which have the capacity to reach deep into their respective traditions and find the strength to reach out to each other.

1. American journalist Daniel Pearl was abducted by terrorists in Pakistan in January, 2002, and murdered on February 21.

The Abuse of Islamic Language

The organizers of the Miss World 2002 pageant in Nigeria were duly chastised for planning a swimsuit spectacle during the month of Ramadan in a country with a sizable Muslim majority; weaknesses in the Nigerian government were exposed for its failing to anticipate and contain deep-seated religious tensions between Muslims and Christians; *ThisDay* columnist Isioma Daniel and her editors were criticized for making light of Muslim protests with insensitive comments about Prophet Muhammad; and the mob violence initiated by a segment of Nigerian Muslims was rightly condemned.

But then, just as the situation calmed, the deputy governor

of Zamfara state issued a fatwa (religious edict) calling for the death of Ms Daniel. At this point, what had been responsible media treatment froze, as if hypnotized by "that" word, leaving a North American public largely uninformed about the criticism of the fatwa by other Muslims, and about its revocation.

Religious authorities in Egypt and Saudi Arabia condemned the fatwa as having no sound basis in Islamic jurisprudence, and Nigeria's supreme Islamic body ordered Muslims to ignore the edict, noting that the state had no religious authority in the first place. For many in the West, however, a fatwa remained, and remains, synonymous with murderous zealotry. In this case, as in others, media focus gave undue credibility to unqualified authorities, while legitimate voices, trained in the rigours of Islamic law, were ignored.

Chronic abuse of Islamic terminology can only contribute to the widening gulf between the "West" and the Muslim world. Whereas Muslims attach a rich, historical legacy to words such as fatwa or jihad, current discourse insists on their interpretation on Western terms.

In the Nigerian debacle, unfortunately titled "Jihad versus Miss World"—a play on Benjamin Barber's 1992 *Jihad vs McWorld*—the use of "jihad" was meant to capture the anger of Nigeria's Muslims. As Mr Barber himself acknowledged, jihad "is a rich word whose generic meaning is 'struggle'— usually the struggle of the soul to avert evil" and that "strictly applied to religious war, it is used only in reference to battles where the faith is under assault." Ironically, Mr Barber insisted on using his own—not the traditional—interpretation, arguing, "My use here is rhetorical, but does follow both journalistic practice and history." This approach was echoed in his 2001 essay "Ballots vs Bullets," in which jihad is understood not as part of Islamic tradition but as "disintegrative tribalism and reactionary fundamentalism."

In 1999, then-chief justice Antonio Lamer of the Supreme Court of Canada issued a public rebuke of those demanding more severe sentences and tougher laws for violent crimes, referring to these concerns as a jihad against justice, apparently oblivious to his own antonymic use of the term.

But misuse of Islamic terminology is not confined to the West. Osama bin Laden has sanctified mass murder by his use of such terms as fatwa and jihad and by deviously manipulating the rich legacy of these concepts. Such misappropriation of Islamic terms requires Muslims to step forward and reclaim the authenticity of their own language. The nihilism of Osama bin Laden is not jihad but *hirabah*, the most loathsome of crimes, in that it involves killing with terror and intimidation.

That is how six of the most respected Muslim scholars described the attacks of September 11, 2001 in a fatwa: "These terrorists' acts, considered by Islamic law [constitute] the crime of hirabah." A prominent Islamic jurist described the bombing in Bali, Indonesia, in October 2002 as "total barbarism ... or hirabah ... a crime in Islam for which severe punishment is specified."[1] Most Islamic scholars say that the principal reason for legislating a jihad is in cases of hirabah— because jihad is meant to be a defence against the senseless harm and targeting of innocents.

The Koran refers to the power of language: a good word is analogous to a tree, with firm roots in the ground, spreading its branches to the heavens, providing fruit and shelter to many. A harmful word is akin to a sickly plant, with shallow roots, yielding bitter fruit.

We can continue to use superficial, injurious terminology to the detriment of many. Or we can insist on using accurate language, firmly rooted in universal concepts that nourish the desire for fair and frank debate.

---

1. http://www.islamonline.net/english/news/2002-0/15/article33.shtml.

Reforming Islam

The 9/11 mass murder jolted Americans to the reality that ignorance of their government's foreign policy was not bliss. Some asked, "Why do the terrorists hate us?" Others blithely answered, "Because we love freedom." How to manage the hate? Call in Madison Avenue to "sell" America to skeptical Muslims around the world. After all, image is everything. The campaign failed miserably, especially after the invasion of Iraq.

The 9/11 Commission report released July 22, 2004, examines possible US responses to threats posed by "Islamist terrorism." Its authors point out that military excursions, while important, will be secondary to the ideological battle against the extremist interpretations of Islam espoused by al-Qaeda and its ilk. It's not that Muslims find such interpretations appealing, but that the genius of Osama bin Laden has been his ability to speak forcefully to the anger and humiliation felt by Muslims because of American intervention in their affairs.

According to the Commission, the United States should do a better job of selling American values to Muslims worldwide through mass media and academic and cultural exchanges. Incredibly, it is silent on the questions of educating Americans about Islam.

The report characterizes the roots of al-Qaeda's ideology as "a long tradition of extreme intolerance within a minority strain of Islam," thereby suggesting that the faith itself has always been a source for extremism. It claims that the enemy is not Islam, but "Islamism"—a nebulous term that defies exact definition. The distinction between Islam and Islamism will be lost on most people, thus providing ample opportunity for exploitation by Islamophobes.

The need for reformation within the Muslim world is pointed out. The argument made is deceptively simple: the prime reason for violence in the name of Islam is that Islam has not changed since its inception. To eliminate the threat of terror, Islam must modernize itself so that its adherents can join the ranks of the "civilized."

There are two problems with this approach. The first is that it ignores centuries of scholarship within Islam itself that seeks to ensure that principles of the faith are able to address issues of modernity. We often hear that Islam divides the world into the "House of Islam," where Muslims dominate, and the "House of War," where Muslims want to dominate. But too infrequently do we hear about Muslim scholars who have rejected this binary world view, arguing instead that a genuine Islamic vision supports a global cooperative model rather than a unilateral state-centric one. Such scholarship sits squarely in the mainstream of Islam.

Secondly, the assumption underlying the argument for reformation is that, once "reformed," the new Islamic outlook will be subservient to the wishes of the civilized West. Yet sovereign nations make sovereign decisions, such as refusing to join in unjust wars and doing what is best for their own economies rather than what is best for an alien power.

Given the stakes, it seems improbable that the United States will remain a bystander in the reformation efforts. A Rand Corporation report (2004) suggests ways in which to engineer Islamic reform by advocating support for secularists, even though such leaders are often autocratic and repressive, and using traditionalists to keep the extremists in check. Thus, the study attempts to pigeonhole 1.6 billion Muslims into distinct groups based on their degree of Islamic practice and interpretation of key Islamic texts. It is reductionist and arrogant, with cultural domination its final goal. Positions of this sort lead Muslims to one conclusion: The call for reformation is not genuine. It has at its heart a vision of Muslims as consumers, not producers; of Muslim nations as liege states rather than equal partners.

The 9/11 report, however, does strike one positive chord: "Islam is not the enemy. It is not synonymous with terror. Nor does Islam teach terror. . . . Lives guided by religious faith, including literal beliefs in holy scriptures, are common to every religion, and represent no threat to us. . . .

"With so many diverse adherents, every major religion will spawn violent zealots. Yet understanding and tolerance among people of different faiths can and must prevail."

The Virtuous Jihad

His is one of the most influential voices among Arab Muslims today.

Exiled by his own country, Egypt, he spreads his message via satellite TV, the Internet, and MP3 files. His taped speeches sell out in the markets of Damascus, Amman, and Cairo. His call for an internal jihad has spurred many to tears and to action. Yet he is virtually unknown to Osama-fixated Westerners.

His name is Amr Khaled; in 2002, *The Economist* described him as "the most fashionable face of the faith." An accountant by training, Mr Khaled underwent a spiritual reawakening during Ramadan a few years ago. Before long, his charismatic style attracted the attention of Cairo's urbane, upper-class youth. In 2000, he hosted *Words from the Heart*, an interactive

TV show devoted to discussion and testimonials about God's love and mercy in daily life.

He made Islamic teachings simple, compassionate, and relevant, in contrast to the harsh rhetoric of other clerics. Dapper in a casual suit, with a trim mustache, he presents a face of Islamic piety rarely seen in the Middle East. Mr Khaled asserts spiritual identity in harmony with the modern world. Think of Deepak Chopra and Billy Graham combined.

His message to Muslims is simple: Reconnect to God through sincerity, humility, and awareness of God's all-encompassing mercy in personal experiences. He gently reminds his audience about the Koranic message that success lies in the purification of the soul—the more virtuous jihad alluded to by the Prophet Muhammad.

Many have taken his message to heart. Female Egyptian entertainers who once scoffed at the hijab now appear veiled on his show to give personal testimonials. Emphasizing less materialism, more spirituality, less ritual, more sincerity, Mr Khaled's genius is to find a middle ground between modernity and Islamic principles.

Most important, he reminds his followers that individual responsibility is paramount, and that each person has the wherewithal to change things for the better. Mr Khaled has launched many successful community projects, much like Oprah's Angel Network. My friends describe how their previous despair and idleness have been replaced by an inner dynamism to improve the world through acts of charity.

So why is he regarded as dangerous in his native Egypt?

One rumour has it that the secular regime was embarrassed when President Hosni Mubarak's daughter-in-law began wearing the Islamic head scarf after hearing Mr Khaled. A more likely explanation is that the state cannot control or co-opt Mr Khaled's growing influence, or cope with his throwing a wrench into the government's plan to designate Islamic activists into two mutually exclusive camps: the bearded, harsh, anti-Western extremists bent on political overthrow versus the austere, state-sanctioned scholars of al-Azhar University. A sizable group is turned off by both, and Mr Khaled fills the void.

Forced to leave Egypt in 2002, he settled at the University of Wales, where he worked on a PhD thesis comparing the Prophet Muhammad's model for social reform to Western models. He broadcasts weekly to the Middle East on Arab satellite TV, while travelling on the Muslim Arab lecture circuit. In Canada, he drew overflowing crowds in Toronto, Montreal, and Ottawa.

A parallel trend, meanwhile, is under way in Pakistan. Its central figure at first glance seems to be Mr Khaled's antithesis. Farhat Hashmi is a mother of four who wears a niqab (face veil) in public. With her background in classical Islamic theology and a PhD from the University of Glasgow, she strongly felt the need to give Muslim women the tools to study primary Islamic sources for themselves. What began as a small study circle grew into an institute, and her public lectures in Urdu drew throngs of women—especially from the Pakistani upper classes. Her taped sermons sell out in Houston, Toronto, and Karachi. Her recent Canadian tour drew huge crowds.

Ms Hashmi's soothing style articulates a message of personal reform. She reminds listeners of God's mercy and forgiveness—in stark contrast to the dire warnings of hellfire favoured by many mullahs, who (not surprisingly) see her as a threat. Her followers are young educated women disenchanted with the spiritual emptiness of Western feminism.

The Islamic "revival" amongst the Westernized Muslim upper classes isn't that puzzling. "Having it all" doesn't mean having "it"—inner tranquillity and a sense of purpose—especially in an age of civilizational tension. In the West, the spiritual is strictly demarcated from the material. Islamic ethos emphasizes a spiritual foundation from which all other activities flow. Many Muslims are harking back to their spiritual roots in search of identity, meaning, and self-fulfilment.

The popularity of reformers such as Mr Khaled and Ms Hashmi demonstrates clearly that a message based on compassion and personal accountability elicits a far greater response from Muslims than hate-filled rhetoric.

The Seduction of Terror: How to Counter It

We thought we were immune. We are not a hated superpower. We did not go to Iraq. Our multiculturalism policy seems light years ahead of Europe's dysfunctional immigration policies. We're nice. We're Canadian. Why would anyone want to commit murder and mayhem on our soil?

Yet that is precisely what eighteen individuals—all homegrown—were allegedly preparing to do, here, in Canada, before being thwarted by security services.[1] The frightening spectre of al-Qaeda-inspired terrorism is now a domestic reality.

The little information that has emerged is disturbing in many respects. A handful of those arrested were under eighteen, while the majority were in their twenties. Young, impressionable minds, ostensibly filled with jihadi fantasies, had allegedly gone from trash talk to "walk the walk." They had never set foot in Afghanistan, Chechnya, Kashmir, or Iraq. How, then, did they become radicalized?

During the brutal occupation of Afghanistan in the 1980s, news of the jihad against the Soviets spread through magazines, videotapes, and first-hand accounts. Recruits volunteered to travel to Afghanistan to fight, and financial aid and military know-how were provided by the US and the Saudis, in their common goal to stop Soviet expansion.

Then came Bosnia. Once again, videos of atrocities committed against Muslims were circulated throughout the world. Many young Muslim men travelled to the former Yugoslavia in defence of their brethren. As Jessica Stern describes in *Terrorism in the Name of God*, the massacre of Bosnian Muslims served as a wake-up call to many European Muslim youth, who saw wholesale murder and rape of their co-religionists go unpunished and unchecked in the heart of Europe.

In both cases, foreign recruits travelled to the centres of conflict to fight for fellow Muslims. Later some of them tried to export their military zeal to start insurgencies in their Arab homelands, only to be brutally suppressed. Others, indigenous to conflict zones—Palestine, Chechnya—took the fight to their occupiers, as a means to avenge humiliation at home.

Then came satellite TV and the Internet, providing horrific images of Muslims maimed and killed in zones of conflict such as Palestine, Kashmir, and Chechnya. Further disturbing images came from Afghanistan, Iraq, Abu Ghraib, and Guantanamo Bay. Throughout, directives flowed in rich Arabic from Osama bin Laden and Ayman al-Zawahri to Muslims. While the West focused on Huntington's "Clash of Civilizations," Ayman al-Zawahri wrote his own tract, calling adherents to fight the "far jihad" (in Western countries), as opposed to the "near jihad" (against Arab governments). The call was to hit the "head of the snake" (the United States), and to recover lost Muslim lands such as al-Andalus (Spain). Some analysts saw the latter as inspiring the Madrid bombings.

Al-Qaeda may have been weakened, but its ideology has

travelled the globe, carried primarily in the minds of young, impressionable Muslims. These young people feel enraged by the oppression of Muslims worldwide, and dissatisfied with the lack of spirituality in modern culture. Seeking a sense of purpose and identity, a fringe finds an outlet in violence. They have seen that a horrific bombing can force a country to withdraw its troops from Iraq (as in Spain), or turn public opinion against its own government's involvement (as in England). Political grievance as motivation is not new. What is new, however, is that the aggrieved are willing to die and take as many people as they can with them.

Canada has been mentioned at least twice on al-Qaeda's hit list. In early 2006, a Taliban official warned the Canadian military to leave Afghanistan or face fierce retribution. In the twisted minds of those who ascribe to this militant ideology, Canada has become fair game. What can be done?

We must work together with the Muslim community to neutralize extremism. At home, this ideology must be fought using counterarguments that are both rational and spiritual in nature, based on the Koran and Prophetic traditions. Imams must continue to denounce extremism at Friday sermons, as they did in a historic national statement last summer in the wake of the London bombings. Ignorance must be countered with sound knowledge and appeals to the conscience.

The politics of grievance, and a resort to minority victim-hood, do little to empower the Muslim community. Despair and helplessness must be met with social projects aimed to help the youth. Elements of the highly successful social projects developed by the Egyption exile Amr Khaled might be developed here. Mr Khaled's programs are rooted in Islamic teachings and provide a sense of identity and greater understanding of the world.

The security agencies and Muslim communities across

Canada must also improve their relationships. The past may have been rocky, with the Maher Arar affair[2] and Project Thread (the ill-fated 2003 police investigation of eighteen Toronto-area Pakistanis and one Indian) sowing much mistrust. However, the threat of terrorism requires continuing effort.[3]

Vilification of an entire group only enhances alienation and mistrust. Provincial and national governments should protect and reassure a community feeling on edge, anticipating a backlash. Muslims on the other hand must continue to take public and private stands against the scourge of terrorism. One way is to hold a public vigil affirming the principles of the highly popular "Not in the Name of Islam" on-line petition, which begins: "We, the undersigned Muslims, wish to state clearly that those who commit acts of terror, murder and cruelty in the name of Islam are not only destroying innocent lives, but are also betraying the values of the faith they claim to represent." Hundreds of thousands have signed.

1. On 2 June, 2006, 17 young men of the greater Toronto area were arrested on terrorism charges; an eighteenth person was arrested in August of that year. Details of the alleged "homegrown" terrorist plot included bombing public buildings and beheading politicians. A controversial aspect of the case was the use of a well-known member of the local Islamic community, who was paid a large sum of money, as an informant. To date, seven members of the 18 have had their charges dropped; one member, a minor when arrested, was found guilty, sentenced to two and a half years in jail, and freed for time already spent. Three have pleaded guilty; and seven are still in custody. (http://www.cbc.ca/canada/toronto/story/2009/09/28/toronto-18-terrorism-guilty482.html).

2. For the Arar affair, see note on p.19.

3. On August 14, 2003, 18 Pakistanis and one from India, were arrested as possible national security threats. In late September of that year, the authorities reversed their decision saying that the men were no longer a security risk or a danger to the public. They were deported. (http://www.cbc.ca /canada/story/2003/11/17/deported031117.html).

Bin Laden vs The Prophet (1):
A War of Ideas

The threat from al-Qaeda and its offshoots remains high, according to US intelligence reports. Osama bin Laden's message continues to attract adherents. In order to understand the power of his ideas, one should study the words of the man himself. Bruce Lawrence, a Duke University Islamicist, has done just that in *Messages to the World*, a compilation of bin Laden's statements from 1988-2004. The recurring theme in bin Laden's arguments is reciprocity.

According to Michael Sheuer, a former CIA agent who was in charge of hunting down bin Laden, al-Qaeda's attacks on the West are not based on "who we are," but because of "what we do" in foreign lands. Mr Sheuer is highly critical of American leaders for lying to the American people about al-Qaeda's true motivation.

In *Messages,* bin Laden lambastes the United States for meddling in the affairs of Muslims. His call: Get out, stop stealing our resources (namely oil), and stop propping up autocratic regimes that act against the interests of the masses. Why, he asks, is Muslim blood so cheap, that it flows so readily in so many lands? His warning: If you continue to kill civilians in our countries, we will do the same in yours, until you stop.

While the vast majority of Muslims reject that prescription, they agree with the gist of the argument—namely, that Western foreign policy has been both intrusive and oppressive. At the heart of Muslim resentment is American support of Israel at the expense of the Palestinians (and, in 2006, the Lebanese). Anger grew, as well, while US troops were stationed for a decade in Saudi Arabia, host of Islam's holiest sites. It reached a tipping point with the invasion of Iraq, the Guantanamo prison abuses, and a "war on terror" that many see as a front for a "war on Islam." Many also see the oft-repeated call for democracy by Western governments as sheer hypocrisy, since people's choices in some Muslim countries have been annulled (Algeria) or punished (Palestine) when they don't conform to the wishes of Washington, Paris, and London.

Osama bin Laden elaborates on these themes using the concept of jihad. What does this mean for Canadians?

Bin Laden specifically mentioned Canada after the United States and its allies, including Canada, attacked Afghanistan in 2002. His message to the allies was: do not support the US in its hegemonic enterprises. Our fight is with the Americans, but if you insist on supporting their aims by invading our lands, then we will bring the fight to you in yours.

The ramifications of the Afghan mission on domestic security have yet to enter into public debate. However, the trials and the testimonies of the eighteen Toronto-area men accused of planning a terror campaign[1] should shed further light. Media accounts have suggested that the men felt resentful of Canada's military presence in Afghanistan.

This does not mean that our foreign policy should be held hostage to terror. However, we need to recognize that there is mounting anger—especially amongst Muslim youth—at the injustices perpetrated against their coreligionists elsewhere. When it comes to Afghanistan, there is dismay at the high number of civilian deaths at the hands of NATO forces; the impunity with which warlords continue to operate; and the impression that Hamid Karzai is yet another Western puppet. Bin Laden's message of reciprocity—cloaked in powerful religious terminology—is taking root.

In order to diffuse this trend toward an extremist response, we must adopt a strategy that has legitimacy both in the language of Islam, and in democratic norms. In *Messages*, bin Laden acknowledges that the Prophet Muhammad forbade the killing of innocent civilians in combat. Yet, to support his call for violence in the West, he bypasses the Prophet's words in favour of the rulings of a medieval scholar, Ibn Taymiyyah, who sanctioned the killing of noncombatants. Bin Laden stresses reciprocity and perpetual warfare, whereas the Prophetic template stressed patience, strict limits on war, and amnesty.

Therefore, in the battle of ideas, Muslim scholars must counter bin Laden's arguments with authoritative Prophetic examples. In the social sphere, there needs to be a push towards civic engagement by Muslim youth. This means that Islamic centres must stop importing preachers who encourage isolation and who forbid or discourage voting. At the same time, Muslim youth should have legitimate avenues to vent grievances and engage politicians. The Americans recognized the importance of this approach by sponsoring a National Muslim American Youth Summit, in which Muslim youth met officials from the departments of Homeland Security, State and Justice. We should follow that example in Canada.

Finally, Muslim youth have the shining examples of Maher Arar and Monia Mazigh, who persevered against terrible injustice without falling prey to radicalization or hatred. Mr Arar has even called for rebuilding public trust in the very institutions that failed him. Their inspiring story is the ultimate lesson in civic engagement.[2]

1. see note on p.16.

2. Maher Arar, a Canadian citizen born in Syria in 1970, came to Canada in 1987. He holds a bachelor's and a master's degree in computer engineering, and worked in Ottawa as a telecommunications engineer. During a stopover in New York while returning to Canada from a vacation in Tunisia

in September 2002, Arar was detained by US officials claiming he had links to al-Qaeda. He was deported to Syria, and returned to Canada a year later, claiming he had been tortured with American approval. Arar's wife Monia Mazigh holds a PhD in financial economics.

According to a *Globe and Mail* article, "Maher Arar is an innocent victim of inaccurate RCMP intelligence reports and deliberate smears by Canadian officials, a commission of inquiry says in a report that also recommends the federal government pay him compensation . . . 'The RCMP provided American authorities with information about Mr Arar which was inaccurate, portrayed him in an unfair fashion and overstated his importance to the investigation,' the report says . . . " (http://www.the globeandmail.com/news/national/article843751.ece)

In 2009, Mr Arar was finally awarded a $10.5 million settlement by the Canadian government and given a full apology by the prime minister, Stephen Harper.

Bin Laden vs The Prophet (2): Two Opposing Visions for Canadian Muslims

After the Battle of Uhud, fought in 625 between the nascent Muslim community of Medina and the powerful Meccan army, the Prophet Muhammad and his followers scoured the battlefield to see who had been martyred during combat. They came across the Prophet's uncle, Hamza, whose body lay mutilated. Hamza was a powerfully built man with the spirit of a lion, one of the few prominent converts to Islam during its early years. His mutilation was courtesy of a woman named Hind, wife of the Meccan chief. Her hatred of Muslims was so deep that she had ordered Hamza's belly to be slit and proceeded to chew his liver.

It was in this state that the Prophet found his beloved uncle. Angered by the sheer barbarity of the act, he vowed revenge on the Meccan community. His companions concurred, promising a massacre "like the Arabs had never seen before." Retribution pulsed through their veins.

And then, according to theological sources, the Prophet received a revelation from God to be patient, to confront injustice with justice. Retaliation against civilians was out of the question.

You will never find this key incident mentioned in the speeches of Osama bin Laden, or the Internet exhortations of those bent on mayhem and murder in the name of Islam. They will all evoke Muhammad's name, but they will rarely cite his example. They will cloak their murderous intentions in the mantle of jihad to provide legitimacy for their terror. But theirs is not a path of jihad—it is a path of hirabah (barbarism). We should refrain from calling them jihadis.

Current hirabi aspirations are stoked by perceived and real injustices inflicted on Muslims around the world. While the majority of Muslims do not share the destructive vision of extremists, there is a groundswell of popular resentment against Western (notably American) interventions in Muslim lands, and the accompanying dirty geopolitical games. Abu Ghraib, Guantanamo Bay, extraordinary renditions and the immoral war in Iraq have done nothing but increase the Muslim masses' contempt for the United States.

As we read about the trials of Muslim terrorism suspects now under way,[1] we realize how deep this resentment can run: these Western-raised Muslim youths had allegedly planned to murder fellow citizens in retaliation. Against the edicts of the Koran and the example of Muhammad, they chose to follow the path of Osama bin Laden.

Many Canadian Muslims are in a state of shock at the revelations and slowly awakening from a state of denial. Their cynicism is rooted in incidents involving Muslims in Canada: the complicity of the RCMP and the Canadian Security Intelligence Service in the Maher Arar affair;[2] the sensationalist and apparantly erroneous branding of eighteen illegal Pakistani immigrants (and one Indian) as a "terror cell" in 2002;[3] the detention of noncitizens under secret evidence now deemed unconstitutional.[4] Years of publication bans on information pertaining to the arrests in Ottawa and Toronto have provided fertile ground for conspiracy theories based on ethno-religious profiling.

It is public disclosure of information that offers the best arguments against these one-sided views. As evidence is presented and rebutted, a more complete picture emerges, thereby challenging assumptions and awakening people to the blood lust of those professing jihad, to the hate of humanity pervading chat rooms, to the contempt that these young extremists have for their fellow Muslims.

One can oppose foreign policy through existing democratic channels without resorting to violence. This path requires patience and justice—like that displayed by the Prophet. As Peter Bergen noted in *The New Republic*, the real, battle-hardened jihadis are beginning to confront the hirabis on their own turf with the stark immorality of their nihilistic visions. But every Muslim has a responsibility to confront the hate espoused by these hirabis. Silence is not an option.

A few blocks from the Ottawa courthouse where Momin Khawaja faced terrorism charges related to the London attacks,[5] Parliament Hill played host in 2008 to a symposium titled "Cosmopolitan Identity in the Islamic World." The meeting's purpose was to create dialogue between Western policy-makers and Muslim thinkers, counteract misperceptions, and facilitate Muslims' contributions to their societies, based on the rich history of Islamic thought.

The contrast between the two events could not have been starker. Each represents a metaphor for the vision of Islam. One involves engagement, dialogue, and confidence in universal paradigms rooted in Islamic thought. The other presents a vision rooted in hate, death, and destruction. The choice couldn't be clearer.

1. see note on p.16.
2. see note on p.19.
3. see note on p.16.
4. see article "Canadian Double-talk" on p.52.
5. Momin Khawaja, a software engineer, was arrested in March 2004 on terrorism related charges. He was convicted in March 2009 and sentenced to 10 ½ years in jail.

Acknowledging Fanaticism

Transcripts show that the American jury in the trial of Zacarias Moussaoui, a wannabe 9/11 highjacker, had heard the gut-wrenching cockpit recording of the last half-hour of United Airlines Flight 93. Throughout the mayhem, the hijackers invoked "Allah, the Greatest" many times as they prepared to send all those aboard to a violent, gruesome death. The act of mass murder is evil; invoking the name of God makes it all the more repulsive.

The hijackers had all met and trained in al-Qaeda camps in Afghanistan. This is the same land where, twenty-five years ago, the Soviets also used airplanes to murder innocent civilians—sometimes by throwing them off an aircraft in midflight. Such incidents spurred many Afghans to fight against the Soviets. Unfortunately, some went beyond the strict norms of jihad, choosing to adopt a militant ideology. Cherry-picking verses from the Koran, they used God to justify criminal behaviour and, in the end, acted no better than the Soviets.

There has been concern that publication of the Flight 93 transcripts, along with the release of the film *United 93*, may contribute to Islamophobia. Yet isn't it more honest to acknowledge the rising tide of fanaticism, dissect its deviancy and vigorously disavow its ideology? Facile rejoinders such as "Islam is peace" are ineffectual and incredible, in light of so much violence being wrought—albeit by a tiny minority—in the name of our religion.

Which brings us to the case of Abdul Rahman, an Afghan convert to Christianity. In March 2006, his own family "outed" him to authorities during a nasty custody dispute. Afghan clerics summarily called for his execution as punishment for apostasy, citing Islamic law. The reaction by Muslims in North America and other parts of the world could not have been more contrary. Individuals, various groups, and legal scholars all called for the unconditional release of Mr Rahman, affirming both freedom of religion and freedom of conscience as fundamental tenets of Islam. The Koran states that "there is no compulsion in religion." While apostasy is disapproved of in the Koran, no punishment is prescribed for it. There are also many examples of apostates being brought before the Prophet (including his personal scribe) who were left unharmed. Renunciation of faith, unaccompanied by sedition or treason, did not warrant punitive action.

Islamic laws regarding apostasy were developed more than a thousand years ago, during vastly different political and social conditions. At the time, Muslim identity was inextricably linked to the Islamic empire. As such, apostasy was often seen as the equivalent of treason against the state. This situation is not unlike the example given by novelist Leila Aboulela in *The Translator*: A British soldier, stationed in Egypt during the Second World War, converts to Islam and finds he can't return home. Given the political and social climate of Britain at the time, his conversion is regarded as treason.

Perhaps the Afghan response to apostasy should also be

viewed against the backdrop of the brutal invasions that have formed part of that nation's history. But Muslims are by no means a monolithic entity; the manner in which Islam is practised differs from nation to nation. What emerges from Afghanistan as "Islamic" should be weighed against practices in the wider Muslim world. The Taliban banned education for girls, and was the only government of a predominantly Muslim country to do so. Over the past decade, Kuwait has had one of the world's highest female literacy rates, paving the way for a robust suffragette movement. And while Afghan women are making inroads in the current political system, Muslims have already elected female heads of government in Pakistan, Bangladesh, and Indonesia.

Living in Fear:
Canadian While Muslim

Don't Shackle Us to 9/11

Verily, with hardship, comes ease.
Indeed, verily with hardship, comes ease.

—*Koran*, Surah 94, Verses 5-6

These verses from the Koran are most apt to describe the reality of recent years for Canadian Muslims, and the guarded optimism of those with faith.

Since September 11, 2001, many Canadian Muslims have experienced what can aptly be described as their *annus horribilis*. The events of that fateful day were traumatic enough—defenseless civilians of every faith, age and race, mercilessly slaughtered while going about their daily routines in the heart of North America. Canadian Muslims, like everyone else, were horrified. However, the brief unity in grief soon gave way to fearful isolation, once it became known that the perpetrators committed this heinous act in the name of Islam.

Canadians of the Muslim faith instinctively knew that they would become the subject of collective guilt in their own country. Many took precautions by keeping their children home from school, and staying out of the public eye. Muslim institutions called on the police for protection.

Community organizations and imams condemned 9/11 in the strongest possible terms as antithetical to Islam. Still, that did not stop those committed to venting their blind anger. Taunts, threats, physical assaults, and vandalism against personal property and Muslim institutions were recorded by police units across the country within the first months after

9/11. The Council on American-Islamic Relations Canada (CAIR-CAN) released the results of a poll about how Canadian Muslims have fared in the year since that fateful day. Of nearly 300 respondents, 60 percent indicated that they had been subject to some form of discrimination or bias, while 80 percent indicated they knew of someone else who had been subject to the same.

As the spike in documented hate crimes faded after two months, Canadian Muslims felt a more insidious form of discrimination: that of a community under suspicion. A few media commentators brazenly categorized Muslims as a "fifth column," hiding sleeper cells amongst their midst. Others questioned their loyalty as Canadian citizens. Bordering on hate literature, some columns and national editorials dehumanized Muslims as a barbaric, murderous people.

Trial by media, guilt by religious identity, seemed to be the norm as the Canadian public was treated to a spectacle of Muslims paraded by the RCMP as "prime suspects": a nuclear engineer of Egyptian origin at the Atomic Energy of Canada, whose alleged wrongdoing was based on having a name similar to that of lead hijacker Mohamed Atta; an Ottawa man originally from Somalia who managed wire transfers for Canadians sending money to support their families in Somalia; a Toronto copy shop owner who was also the uncle of the infamous Nabil al-Marabh. Full of sound and fury, these dramatic announcements were found later to signify nothing. Lives had been devastated by irresponsible actions of the media and the RCMP.

Despite the exposure of these glaring errors made by the intelligence authorities, Muslims have remained under a cloud of suspicion. An IPSOS-Reid poll in 2002 indicated that 35 percent of Canadians were more suspicious of Arabs and Muslims from the Middle East, an 8 percent increase since the poll asked the same question on September 21, 2001. And 48 percent of Canadians also indicated that they favoured some form of racial profiling.

Perhaps the deepest offence, though, were the attacks against Islam itself. A few commentators have relished the opportunity to display their ignorance by imputing 9/11 to the Koran itself (even in the pages of *The Globe and Mail*, where one columnist referred to verses of warfare as proof that violence is the foundation of Islam, and another branded the Egyptian murderer of El Al airline employees at Los Angeles airport as a "devotee of the Koran.") Call-in radio shows provided a snapshot of the mindset of people openly hostile to the faith itself.

Given this, will Canada's unique multicultural foundation be eroded as openness gives way to suspicion; inclusion replaced by enclaves of disaffected minorities; transparency of justice clouded by secret evidence and secret trials?

Those and subsequent events have forced many Muslims to explain their faith to the wider public. This is a responsibility that the community should have borne long ago. It has also led to introspection, and in many instances to a strengthening of faith and identity. And it has exposed fundamental differences within the community regarding the interpretation of religious teachings and its role here in Canada.

Now, more than ever, Koranic words of solace, inspiration, and divine care are helping individuals cope day to day, combating uncertainty with unshakable faith, the cloud of suspicion with rays of divine light, and betrayal of confidence in human beings with firm reliance in the compassionate Almighty.

As Canadian Muslims look to the near past, they discover that many ethnic groups have gone through similar trials: Ukrainians and Poles during the First World War; Germans, Italians, and Japanese during the Second World War, and Jews during the first half of the past century. By fighting discrimination, each group emerged stronger, with its role further entrenched in the Canadian mosaic.

Canadian Muslims must come to terms with the reality that it is now their turn. Will they fight discrimination and challenge violations to civil rights, thus contributing toward the evolution of social justice in Canada? Will they consolidate their great reservoir of talent and values into instruments of change for the benefit of all? Or will they retreat into ghettos, contributing to the vicious cycle of mutual suspicions between "civilizations"?

Social harmony, however, is a two-way street. And the results of the CAIR-CAN poll provide optimism: More than 60 percent of Canadian Muslims report acts of kindness and support by their fellow citizens in the wake of 9/11. Numerous interfaith dialogues, town-hall meetings, and open houses are evidence of the spontaneous outreach extended by fellow Canadians. It is this wellspring of basic human goodness that must continue to flow for the preservation of social cohesion. The media have a responsibility in fostering understanding between peoples, without compromising their role as a forum to probe sensitive issues.

Canadian while Muslim

First, there was "driving while black," the expression that summarized racial profiling often employed by American police. Then came "flying while Arab" to denote the suspicion that followed 9/11. Now, since the arrest of eighteen alleged terrorists in Toronto, we have "Canadian while Muslim."

Reaction to the arrest of the Toronto eighteen[1] has ranged from the sublime (rescind multiculturalism) to the ridiculous (ban burkas). Racist language and thinly veiled Islamophobia have laced media commentaries. One columnist said the young men arrested were "bearded in the Taliban fashion," though the facial hair, based on courtroom drawings, looked similar to beards sported by hockey players during NHL play-offs. Suspects were often described as "brown skinned," and there frequently followed the mantras of "homegrown threat" and "the enemy within."

It is interesting to note that Michael Sandham, a former police officer and soldier-turned-Bandido member, has yet to be described as "white skinned," a "homegrown threat" (he's a Canadian charged with the murder of eight men), or an "enemy within" (he was a Bandido-friendly police officer). Double standards abound. Welcome to the world of "Canadian while Muslim."

Yet, we cannot give in to cynicism. "Canadian while Muslim" puts an onus on Muslims to work twice as hard—to fight extremism on the one hand and Islamophobia on the other. It is heartening to see individuals and groups stepping forward to take on this social responsibility, each in their own way. Muslims, after all, are not a monolith.

Recently, the CBC's *The Current* featured Saira Absar, a working mother expecting her second child who became increasingly frustrated at the negative portrayal of Islam. The Toronto arrests were the last straw. She works in the TSX building that was allegedly targeted. Her son is cared for by her in-laws, who happened to live near one of the individuals arrested. It was too close to home. Taking matters into her own hands, Saira has decided to wage her own jihad—struggle—against those who have perverted the faith. It is her personal mission and responsibility.

Saira has reminded imams of their responsibility to educate congregants about the true nature of Islam. She has warned youth and adults. For Saira, parents have the most pivotal role, since they carry the moral authority to dissuade. Their warnings against drugs, gangs and guns must now include warnings against extremism. All this effort in the eighth month of pregnancy? "It's the best time to do it," says Saira. "You are bringing a new life into this world. The responsibility is even greater now than ever before, I don't want my children to grow up with Islam holding them back. I don't want them to be pointed out at airports, in schools, or in their workplace. That is going on right now."

In Victoria, curator Astri Wright put together a stirring art exhibit, titled *Seeker, Sentry, Sage: Shades of Islam in Contemporary Art*, which featured the works of fifteen Canadian Muslim artists. Some are multigenerational Canadians, while others arrived a few decades ago. The show was a delight for both the soul and the eyes. While the exhibit had been planned well before the Toronto arrests, it could not have come at a better time. Artists from a variety of cultural backgrounds had created original works that touched upon issues of East and West, sacred and secular, past and present. Each had drawn upon the rich legacy of Islamic art and culture spanning fourteen centuries. This exhibit was a testimony to the richness of human experience that flourishes in our Canadian mosaic.

Another example of social responsibility is the so-called Summit on Extremism proposed by a coalition of national Muslim groups. The idea goes beyond feel-good marches or vigils. Instead, it rests on the foundation of shared citizenship. Muslims, as Canadian citizens, are stepping forward to work with Canadian institutions to tackle the problem of extremism. "We will do our part, but we can't do it all alone. Let's work together to make our communities, our nation, safer" is the resounding message. These examples are all signs of maturation in a community suffering from fear and uncertainty. It is the staunch commitment to universal principles that will entrench it into the fabric of Canadian society.

1. see note 1 on p.16.

Living with Fear

Canada is obviously not immune from the madness of terrorism. There have been reports of sleeper cells prepared to mount synchronized bombings in Britain, France, Italy, Belgium, and Canada. Ward Elcock, former director of the Canadian Security Intelligence Service, has warned that a terrorist strike on Canadian soil is not a question of "if," but "when."

And yet, if there is one segment of Canadian society that has lived with the constant fear of terrorist attacks, it is Canadian Muslims and Arabs. They know they will bear the brunt of the fallout.

The fear-mongering was in full swing when a prominent *Globe and Mail* columnist warned us that "your average terrorist is likely to look and sound a lot like the guy next door."[1] Some have placed the onus solely on Muslims to rein in extremists in their midst or risk retribution. If they don't, wrote Thomas Friedman in *The New York Times*, "the West will do it in a rough, crude way—by simply shutting them out, denying them visas and making every Muslim in its midst guilty until proven innocent."[2]

This brutish scenario is based on a similar logic used by extremists to justify their own barbarism against innocent civilians: rein in a foreign policy that approves of rendition, torture, prison abuse, invasion of Muslim lands, and collateral casualties, or we will respond in a rough, crude way that labels every Westerner guilty. With this way of thinking, the cycle of accusation, suspicion and retribution will only continue.

We can only wonder what legislative and policy changes are in the works should an attack occur in Canada. Given Mr Friedman's comments, Muslims have every right to fear the impact. Is internment in the works? Mass deportations of noncitizens? Limits placed on individual rights and freedom of movement? Are there plans to protect Muslims against the ensuing backlash? Our government has been conspicuously silent on its contingency plans.

Poll after poll has shown that Canadian Muslims are viewed with greater suspicion by their fellow Canadians. And yet, no level of government has drawn up a plan to lessen this invisible division, let alone acknowledge this fact. When our government is in denial, what else can this lead to except alienation on the part of Canadian Muslims and Arabs? This alienation can not help in our common fight against extremism.

It is in the interest of all to engage in frank discussions, and to work toward effective means of cooperation. It won't be easy, but it is necessary. Our common security depends on it.

The Muslim community must also look within, and exercise vigilance against hateful rhetoric that masquerades as faith. Greater emphasis must be placed on the universality of Islamic teachings, and the duty before God to work for the welfare of humanity—first locally, then globally. Finally, all members of the community must contribute toward building an ethic of citizenship based on a foundation of civic responsibility. Islamic teachings emphasize that Muslims are to be a source of security and safety for their neighbours.

We live in an age of fragile security. The Muslim community should not be seen as part of the problem, but as a partner in the fight against a common enemy—extremism. We unanimously condemned the bombings in London, joined in interfaith prayers and offered condolences to the families of victims. And yet, the burden we face is greater, because we are a community under suspicion.

We are part of the Canadian fabric, choosing to live in a land envied by many. We are professionals, students, workers, parents trying to raise families. We are your neighbours and coworkers. Any terrorist attack, God forbid, will not differentiate between me and you, between Muslim and not. We are not the "other." Let us join together in our common humanity to stop this madness.

1. *The Globe and Mail,* July 12, 2005.
2. *The New York Times,* July 8, 2005.

Double Standards

A rabbi, a Protestant preacher and an imam are invited to speak in Canada.

The rabbi arrives at the border first. The immigration official asks him about his previous hateful comments about Palestinians. "These quotes were said in a certain context," asserts the rabbi. "Fine," says the minister, "come on in, but don't repeat those words."

The preacher arrives next. He is asked by the minister about previous speeches in which he vilified Muslims, Hindus, and homosexuals. "These quotes were said in a certain context," explains the preacher. "All right, you can enter, but watch what you say," advises the official.

Finally, the imam seeks to enter the country. He is queried about some contemptible speeches he made regarding Jews, Hindus, and homosexuals. "These quotes were taken out of context," explains the imam. To which the official replies: "Canada will not tolerate hate-mongers. Entry denied."

"But you let the rabbi and the preacher enter," protests the imam.

"Sure," says the minister, "some groups have more context than others."

Sarcasm is one way to highlight the double standards applied to the Muslim community. One example of such double standards occured when Ottawa effectively barred Sheikh Riyadh ul-Haq, a Birmingham-based imam, from entering Canada to speak at a Muslim youth conference. (Staff at our high commission in London informed the imam he might be refused entry if he flew to Canada. He chose to address the Toronto assembly by video link instead.)

I don't agree with much of what Sheikh ul-Haq has said—his statements of contempt for Jews and Hindus, who, he says, harbour great hatred for Muslims, and his condemnation of homosexuals—but some of those who attack the man are plain wrong about certain things. It was said, for example, that Sheikh ul-Haq called on Muslims to follow the path of shahadah (martyrdom, in Arabic), when in fact he used the word sahabah (meaning, the companions of the Prophet), a rather large difference.

Sheikh ul-Haq's views may be controversial, but he does not appear to cross the line into hate-speech or incitement to violence, and that's a view seemingly shared by the British government, which has not charged him under its stringent anti-hate laws. As a *Globe and Mail* editorial stated, rather than throwing up a wall to try to keep out his views, it's better to let him be heard, and be challenged.

But the government's heavy-handed approach to deny his entry only fuels the feelings of resentment about the obvious double standards applied against Muslims.

In December, 2000, Israeli Rabbi Binyamin Kahane addressed supporters in Toronto. At the time, Rabbi Kahane was the head of Kahane Chai, designated as a terrorist group by both Israel and the United States. (Canada put Kahane Chai on its terrorism list in June, 2005.) The group advocated the expulsion of all Arabs from Israel, supported Baruch Goldstein, who carried out the massacre of twenty-nine Muslim worshippers at a Hebron mosque, and Rabbi Kahane himself wrote a defence of Yigal Amir, the man who assassinated Yitzhak Rabin. Yet Rabbi Kahane was allowed to enter Canada and promote his ideas, which are far worse than Sheikh ul-Haq's.

Perhaps this was an aberration. Yet the government did not adhere to the very principles it used to keep out the imam, when it allowed Reverend Franklin Graham, (whose incendiary views of Muslims and Hindus are well known), to address congregants in Winnipeg a few months after the imam's cancelled visit. (He came on October 20, 2006).

Rev. Graham, has called Islam "a very evil and wicked religion" and written that "Islam encourages violence in order to win converts and to reach the ultimate goal of an Islamic world." He has said that Hindus are "bound by Satan's power."

The nature of Rev. Graham's words is no different from those of Sheikh ul-Haq. Contempt for the "other" is palpable in both of their screeds.

Speaking of Sheikh ul-Haq, a spokeswoman for Immigration Minister Monte Solberg said "we do not welcome hate-mongers in Canada." Why, then, did the government lay out the welcome mat for Rev. Graham?

And why did those who applauded the government's decision to bar the imam, remain conspicuously silent for Rev. Graham's planned visit?

I suggested to various Muslim organizations that they not oppose Rev. Graham's entry—on the principle that we should not exercise pre-emptive censorship. Let an individual enter, and if he or she violates Canadian law, then prosecute him or her. We must not politicize who is allowed to speak, and who is not.

These are trying times. The arrest of eighteen terrorism suspects in Toronto has led to a rise in Islamophobia, reports the Ontario Human Rights Commission. Given this climate, can we really expect a balanced, nuanced discussion about issues when Muslims are part of the picture?

In one sense, Muslims are going through the quintessential Canadian experience of discrimination. According to historian Jack Granatstein, an anti-immigrant sentiment has long pervaded the nation's psyche. "Whether in the seventeenth century or the twenty-first century, by and large Canadians have always been unhappy with immigration," he said during an interview. "It's always the sense that newcomers aren't like us—they're a problem, they're going to be difficult." Yet history also shows "the extraordinary assimilative force of Canadian society"[1] integrates people into the Canadian fabric.

1. Interview with CTV News, July 2006.

Ugly Then, Ugly Now

Accommodement raisonnable—reasonable accommodation.

It's an oxymoron to some; an object of scorn for Mario Dumont, Official Leader of the Opposition in *la belle province*.

It seems that 400 years of Quebec tradition will not be allowed to be sullied by the religious culture of Jews, Muslims and Sikhs. Not to mention the aboriginal community, whose culture has been decimated by those 400 years of "tradition."

Xenophobia is alive and well in Quebec. Hérouxville[1] was not an aberration, but the canary in a mineshaft. Rather than smother the whiffs of racism, Quebec politicians pandered to the xenophobic fears of voters. For many of Quebec's minorities, "political leadership" is an oxymoron.

So the racism genie is out of the bottle—fuelled and abetted by the media. Call it "manufacturing dissent." More ominously, we witnessed how a media-driven frenzy can give rise to mob rule. Quebec's chief electoral officer felt intimidated enough to scrap a bylaw that allowed registered electors to vote without a photo ID. The object of ire? A few niqabi Muslim women who, themselves, never objected to showing their faces for identification purposes. What the media missed was the generous offer by many Quebeckers to escort these women to polling stations so they could vote free of harassment.

The growing intolerance for accommodation of religious practices in Quebec seems to be reaching a tipping point.

In a 2006 survey, Environics found 53 percent of Quebeckers believed banning the hijab (Islamic head scarf) to be a good idea. The survey did not ask why. Perhaps it's as simple as wanting to follow the example of France. Perhaps they may also want to look to Tunisia, where police actually force women to remove their head scarves on the streets of Tunis, giving new meaning to the expression "fashion police."

Given the spring of discontent with *les accommodements raisonnables*, it will be interesting to see how the public will take to the innovative "ethics and religious culture" curriculum which entered Quebec's primary and secondary schools in 2008. It is not the run-of-the-mill world religions course. Instead, students will have hands-on experience with the world's major religions, aboriginal beliefs and the religious heritage of Quebec. They will study sacred texts and learn the ethos of different world views in order to understand the viewpoints of others.

According to the Quebec Ministry of Education, students should be prepared to live in an increasingly diverse society and cultivate openness to the world. The components of this program—appreciation of Quebec's cultural heritage, openness to others, respect toward people of all beliefs and cooperation—are essential for the formation of a vibrant, peaceful society, according to the ministry.

Let's hope it proceeds.

Is the rest of Canada immune to the fissures emerging in Quebec? It's hard to say. There certainly are tensions between the principle of multiculturalism and that of equality, with the majority of Canadians supporting the latter over the former. The Environics survey shows that roughly one in three Canadians favour banning the hijab (it was one in four a few years ago). With the summer beckoning, how will Canadians react to seeing the four-piece burkini (burka and bikini) at beaches and pools? Some Muslim women, including myself, are choosing the burkini to swim in public while maintaining modesty in attire.

Not familiar with this new fashion? Picture the iconic body suit and cap of Australian gold-medal swimmer Ian Thorpe—with a chic knee-length tunic.

Whether it's the fear of WMDs (women in Muslim dress) or incursions of sharia, the tension really is between Canadians' perception of equality and individual religious freedom. Feminists may rage against the niqab as a symbol of inferiority but, more often than not, Muslim women are freely adopting the veil. Can a uniform view of equality be imposed on everyone?

Of course, there are many positive features to our mosaic. The Environics poll found that Canadian Muslims have a high level of satisfaction with Canada, and this sentiment may actually be on the rise.

The survey was conducted before the announcement of the Maher Arar settlement, before the Supreme Court decision to strike the security certificate legislation, and before the House vote to discontinue controversial provisions of the Anti-Terrorism Act. These resolutions enhanced the trust of Muslims in the Canadian judicial and parliamentary systems.

In fact, it is trust in public institutions, democratic responsibility, and solidarity with fellow citizens that form the basis of "shared citizenship," according to the editors of *Belonging? Diversity, Recognition and Shared Citizenship in Canada*, published in February 2007 by the Institute for Research and Public Policy. These are essential for national cohesion, for they transcend ethnicity, religion, and culture.

Ontario Chief Justice Roy McMurtry writes in the same volume that discrimination and religious/racial profiling undermine social cohesion by whittling away trust and engagement. And while we recognize the corrosive nature of prejudice, perhaps we need to look beyond "tolerance" as the antidote to prejudice.

Researchers at Harvard are touting something called "allophilia" (liking or loving the other) as a more powerful means for social cohesion. Professor Todd Pittinsky believes that some differences between people simply cannot be ignored or eliminated, and the neutral stance of tolerance is not sufficient to keep these differences from festering. Instead, there must be a development of positive attitudes between members of different groups based on trust, admiration, interaction, kinship and ability. He points to Nelson Mandela and Martin Luther King Jr. as leaders who instinctively understood the power of allophilia in countering prejudice.

Given the mood in parts of this country, allophilia seems light years away. A few years ago, Montrealer Gurbaj Singh Multani needed police protection to walk to school through a crowd of jeering, hostile parents. The courts had granted him permission to carry his kirpan to school. The scene was reminiscent of the civil rights era when white parents jeered black students who were bussed to schools in Boston. They were adamantly opposed to children of different races learning together. Today, it's religious practice.

It was ugly then. It's ugly now. What are we going to do about it?

1. In January 2007, the town of Hérouxville, Quebec, passed a code of conduct for immigrants, which included banning the stoning of women and genital mutilation. There are no immigrants in tiny Hérouxville. The *Montreal Gazette* said, "While the values espoused might be universal, the code has sparked an international controversy because the intention appears to be to scare off newcomers with a code that presumes the worst of them." *The Gazette*, February 02, 2007.

It's Still Nasty Out There

In his book *The Gulf Within*, Zuhair Kashmeri documented the painful experiences of Canadian Muslims and Arabs during the 1991 Persian Gulf war. Vandalism, threats, assaults, menacing CSIS interviews, and inflammatory media coverage left an indelible mark on the psyche of an entire community.

This time around, Canadian Muslims and Arabs have not felt the same backlash because of Canada's disengagement from the Iraq conflict and sober public debate about the war's merits.

Yet, prejudice remains a concern. The results of a 2003 survey by the Association for Canadian Studies and Environics Research Group reflect how people perceive the intolerance of others. The survey, which polled 2,002

Canadians between March 15 and 23, showed that concerns over anti-Arab sentiment were harboured by 68 percent, while 30 percent felt Arabs and Muslims project a negative image.

At Concordia University in Montreal, rector Frederick Lowy observed that campus anarchists had "formed an alliance with Muslim students." He told *The Canadian Jewish News* that although "only a small number of Muslim students identify with terrorist groups like Hamas . . . that could change. . . depending on the Muslim political opinion world-wide and the outcome of the Iraq war."[1]

Raising the spectre of a threatening Muslim presence in Montreal, he cited (without basis) a figure of 250,000—an incredible sixfold increase from the official 1991 census figure of 45,000. According to him, pro-Palestinian students had been the principal "aggressors" in tensions at the school. After maligning Muslim students, Mr Lowy issued a tepid apology (some of his comments were misconstrued, etc.), telling them they should feel welcome. He reassured the rest that "there is no evidence that any of our students are terrorists or identify with terrorist organizations."

Ottawa Citizen columnist David Warren was more unequivocal in two lectures he gave at Baylor College in Waco, Texas in early April 2003. The columnist opined that Muslims and Christians have been antagonists since the first time Muhammad declared "Allah is One," denying the Holy Trinity. In the August 2003 Ottawa monthly newsletter *The Christian Current*, he called Islam a "splendidly false" religion.[2]

An anti-Islam conference, scheduled for Kitchener, Ontario, was cancelled after a public outcry. Yet Mark Harding, a self-styled Christian pastor, planned to try again a month later. In 1998, Mr Harding was convicted of inciting hatred against Muslims.

Tussles between certain evangelical groups and Muslims in the United States have had ramifications in Canada. The

Washington-based Council on American-Islamic Relations (CAIR) expressed concern about humanitarian aid to Iraqis by an evangelical charity, the Samaritan's Purse. The group's goal is to convert Muslims to Christianity. Its head, Reverend Franklin Graham, has called Islam "an evil and wicked religion."

An Ontario resident rebuked CAIR for its criticism. Fair enough. But he added: "I am shocked and dismayed by the belief structure being upheld by Muslims in North America where everyone has the freedom of speech and religion. North America was not founded on Muslim principles, else we wouldn't be the strong continent we are today. We would be a backwoods civilization like many Muslim nations found in the Middle East today. I would recommend you work with Christians and Jews, and not against them as your faith would have it. Yeah, we are the infidel, but in North America, thank God you are a minority religion."

The individual turned out to be an executive of a Progressive Conservative riding association. The Canadian office of CAIR brought this matter to the attention of the PC brass. There was added concern because a local mosque had been firebombed after 9/11. Shortly after, the two sides jointly denounced the Islamophobic comments as "absolutely unacceptable," reiterating that they "bear no relation whatsoever to the position and policies of the PC Party of Canada."

We must mend our multicultural mosaic with education about one another—and we must maintain our mosaic by being vigilant against the seeds of hate and exclusion.

1. *The Canadian Jewish News,* March 28, 2003.

2. http://deborahgyapong.blogspot.com/2006/03/david-warren-on-crisis-of-faith.html

Exposing anti-Muslim Discomfort

The endorsement of 2008 Democratic presidential candidate Barack Obama by Colin Powell, former Secretary of State and a Republican, reverberated in the media. But Mr Powell's other endorsement—that of American Muslims—during his interview with NBC's Tom Brokaw went largely unnoticed.

The comments were made in response to the whisper campaign over Mr Obama's alleged Muslim faith. In addition to squashing this rumour, Mr Powell went on to point out the obvious: Mr Obama "is not a Muslim, he's a Christian. He's always been a Christian. But the really right answer is, what if he is? Is there something wrong with being a Muslim in this country? The answer's no, that's not America. Is there something wrong with some seven-year-old Muslim-American kid believing that he or she could be president?"

Mr Powell went on to rebuke anti-Muslim bigotry within senior ranks of the Republican Party, adding: "I have heard senior members of my own party drop the suggestion, 'He's a Muslim and he might be associated [with] terrorists.' This is not the way we should be doing it in America."

Mr Powell then cited the example of Kareem Rashad Sultan Khan, a twenty-year-old American soldier killed by an IED in Iraq in August 2008. Only fourteen at the time of 9/11, he enlisted after high school. Mr Khan was as American as they come—crazy about Disney World, a Dallas Cowboys fan—and wanted to show that not every Muslim was a fanatic and that some would risk their lives for America. On Mr Khan's headstone in Arlington National Cemetery is a crescent and star, along with a list of his military awards—a Purple Heart and a Bronze Star. *The New Yorker* published a haunting picture of his grieving mother at his grave, poignantly illustrating that our common humanity far surpasses our differences.

While the presidential election showcased American resolve to overcome its racist past, it also exposed the lingering discomfort that many Americans feel towards Islam and Muslims. At a town hall-style meeting, an audience member thought Mr Obama was an "Arab." To which Republican nominee John McCain responded: "No, ma'am, he's a decent family man." As if one cannot be both an Arab and a decent family man. Not surprisingly, these prejudices were shamelessly exploited during the election. Yet, as Mr Powell stressed in his interview on NBC, "we have got to stop polarizing ourselves in this way."

It is heartening to see an individual with the stature of Colin Powell stand up to bigotry in the heat of an election. It renews faith in an America that values equality and opportunity for all those who embrace its ideals.

Canadians, like Americans, are uncomfortable with Muslims. According to a Leger Marketing poll published in September 2008, anti-Muslim sentiment is on the rise in Canada, with xenophobic feelings more pronounced in Quebec. While high-profile terrorism trials in Brampton and Ottawa may have contributed to such views, it's a worrisome trend that only enhances marginalization. We need to work harder to bridge an emerging divide based on frank, yet respectful, discussions.

How do we build an inclusive society, where all members feel they are welcome to contribute towards the betterment of self and nation? Our federal political culture, which thrives on denigration and naked partisanship, seems woefully inadequate to adopt the big-tent approach of Mr Obama.

Yet, Canada is seen as a model of multicultural harmony.

As Canadians, let's continue to weave our compassionate meritocracy, based on genuine respect for each and every human being, notwithstanding their values, their beliefs and their origins. In time, we can pave the way towards our own Obama moment: the election of an aboriginal Canadian as prime minister.

Deliver Us from Suspicion

For Muslims, the month of Ramadan is a special time to purify the spirit through fasting, charity and extra prayers. We reflect deeply upon the Koran, expressing gratitude for the many blessings we often take for granted. Whether the favours are tangible (e.g. health, food, shelter) or intangible (peace, personal security), the heartfelt sentiment is best captured by the phrase: "There but for the grace of God go I."

I was waiting in a doctor's office with two flu-ridden children. It was November 11, and at 11 AM the busy staff stopped all work and stood respectfully to a solemn rendition of "O Canada" broadcast on CBC Radio. One silver-haired patient sang with deep conviction. My beautiful country, I thought. A beacon of light in a world filled with so much darkness. One of the few places where a worried mother can get prompt medical attention for her sick children, despite our current health-care concerns.

As we observed two minutes of silence, my six-year-old son asked what was happening. I tried to explain the significance of remembering the efforts of those who had died in conflict.

But it's also important to remember that while Canadian soldiers were fighting tyranny overseas, many were battling the tyranny of discrimination here in Canada. During both world wars, various ethnic groups faced suspicion, even internment, under the pretext of national security. Their treatment was often enshrined in law, later repealed by the efforts of those who found the miscarriage of justice unconscionable. Albertan suffragette Nellie McClung fought on behalf of Japanese Canadians and Jewish refugees during the Second World War. Such struggles have helped the cause of justice in Canada.

In the post-9/11 era, Canadian Muslims and Arabs find themselves a minority under suspicion based on the pretext of national security. The harrowing tale of Maher Arar[1] has evoked collective outrage—more so, given the signs of complicity on the part of Canadian security services.

At least three more Canadians remain in Middle East prisons: Ahmad Abou El Maati in Egypt, and Abdullah Almalki and Arwad al-Boushi in Syria.[2] According to family members, all three were under surveillance by CSIS and the RCMP. Does Canada have its own unofficial "rendition" policy—asking unsavory regimes to pick up Canadian citizens travelling abroad and subject them to torture to break their will?

In Mr Arar's case, it's clear that transcripts of his "confession" found their way back to CSIS in Canada, with portions leaked by "anonymous" government sources. Attempting to smear Mr Arar, they claimed that he had "spilled the beans" on some of the Muslim immigrants imprisoned on secret evidence under Canada's security certificate. Does the Crown's "evidence" include torture-based confessions— evidence that would be rejected under normal rules? Remember; the defendant is not allowed to cross-examine, let alone see the evidence presented against him.

Our immigration department, stinging from American criticism of being too soft, decided to show just how tough it was by publicizing its handling of nineteen Pakistani illegal immigrants. The muscle-flexing was meant for the audience due south. Even justice officials here said there was no evidence of a terrorist conspiracy—just your garden-variety immigration scam. Yet the publicity cast a smear on the lives of these men, and sent a chill through the local Pakistani community. Those deported back to Pakistan have been interrogated about the alleged al-Qaeda link. Our immigration department refuses to admit error or issue an apology.

These are a few of the more public examples of Muslims caught in the dragnet of security zeal. While there have been no terrorist attacks in North America since 9/11, many innocent lives have been ruined. At times of difficulty, Muslims are reminded that "God does not burden any soul beyond what it can bear." Rather than sink into victimhood, they should stand tall and demand fair treatment, following the examples of the struggle by Canada's other ethnic groups.

On the eve of her husband's return from Syria, Monia Mazigh graciously called his release "a victory for Canadian values." Given what we now know, this characterization was premature. There will be no victory until there is a full accounting of the role of government agencies in the suspension of constitutional rights of many Muslims and Arabs.

1. see note 2 on p.19.

2. Abdullah Almalki, Ahmed Al Maati and Muayyed Nureddin all spent time in Syria's most feared prison where they say they were tortured and accused of links to al-Qaeda. All were eventually freed and allowed to return to Canada. Almalki spent 22 months in custody after his arrest in Syria in 2002. He told CBC's *The Current* that his Syrian torturers told him they were getting their information from Canada. Kuwaiti-born El Maati was a truck driver who was tortured in both Egypt and Syria, and told reporters that both countries spoke of getting information about him from Canadian officials. Nureddin was the principal of an Islamic school in Toronto and was arrested at the Syrian border as he was returning from visiting relatives in northern Iraq in 2004.

All three men were investigated by the Canadian Security Intelligence

Service for links to terrorism but were never arrested or had any restrictions placed on their movements in this country. Their lawyers say they were targeted because they were Muslims and knew others who were under CSIS or RCMP investigation.

Former Ottawa resident Arwad al-Boushi, the last of five Canadians imprisoned in Syria, was released in 2007 after nearly 3½ years behind bars.

(http://www.cbc.ca/canada/story/2005/11/07/al-boushi-released 051107.html)

(http://www.cbc.ca/canada/story/2007/03/21/tortureinquiry.html)

Canadian Double-talk

Clifford Olson. Paul Bernardo. Michael Brière. Names of cold-blooded killers that evoke loathing. It seems that our justice system does just fine: catching suspects, laying charges, trying the accused in open court, and confining the guilty to prison. Built into the judicial process is the opportunity for adversarial review—a system of checks and balances to minimize human biases and errors.

Now consider these five names: Hassan Almrei. Adil Charkaoui. Mohamed Zeki Mahjoub. Mahmoud Jaballah. Mohamed Harkat. All non-citizens, all Arab and Muslim. They spent years behind bars. For murder? Terrorism? Pedophilia? Investor fraud?

Actually, we don't know. Neither do they. None was charged with committing any crime. Our government and its security agencies—paragons of transparency and trust— deemed them a threat to national security, and issued a "security certificate" against each. The security certificate allowed the government the right to put each behind bars indefinitely, until he could be deported or charged. Furthermore, he had no right to see the evidence against him, due to "national security"—that catch-all phrase invoked in the name of justice. The men were held in solitary confinement, or incarcerated with hardened criminals, without the right to appeal. They faced deportation to countries where they could be tortured.[1]

Welcome to Canada, post-9/11.

In 2004, Bill Graham, former foreign affairs minister, angrily denounced the secrecy of Iranian officials investigating the death of Canadian Iranian photojournalist Zahra Kazemi. "Under all human-rights codes, under all international law standards, there should be a public trial," he thundered. "Justice will not be done behind closed doors."

Oh really?

Mr Mahjoub is a father of two; Mr Jaballah has six children. National security deemed that a glass wall must suffice to convey the love and affection between these fathers and their children. One of Mr Jaballah's kids said that, if the government did not release his father, he wanted to join him so the two could play together. Mr Mahjoub, detained since June of 2000, went on a hunger strike in a bid to seek contact visits with his wife and children. Neither man had conjugal visits with his spouse. Not one embrace in four years—in the name of national security.

Each woman became a single mother, struggling to make ends meet, in an unfamiliar environment. Let's not forget that these women were shunned because of their husbands' notorious status. As the Arar inquiry showed, associating with intelligence targets could get you deported to a Syrian prison, to be held indefinitely without charge. No wonder many Muslim immigrants are fearful of reaching out to their families. No one wants to be "Arared."

Many notable Canadians came forward to challenge this black hole of justice. Yet, according to a national poll, taken in 2005, the public strongly favoured security over civil liberties.

Some 46 percent of Canadians favoured detaining suspected terrorists without trial, while 62 percent believed Canada should give the US "any information they requested about Canadian citizens whom they suspected of being terrorists."

Astounding statistics regarding attitudes towards people who are suspected—not convicted. We Canadians should drop our smug moral superiority toward the United States, where a Pew poll showed that 62 percent of Americans believed that the US Supreme Court should address the rights of those accused of terrorism.

The Supreme Court decided to hear Mr Charkaoui's argument that the security certificate process violates both our Constitution and international law. Here's the irony: A man deemed a threat to national security used the very system he purportedly sought to destroy.

Some have argued that all five men have been afforded due process. Yet a judge in the Jaballah case has called the process "invidious," describing the detention as Canada's version of Guantanamo Bay. Mr Justice James Hugesson of the Federal Court said, "We hate it. We hate hearing only one party. We hate having to decide what, if any, sensitive material can or should be conveyed to the other party." He added that he sometimes felt "like a fig leaf."

Many legal personalities and organizations have also criticized the lack of adversarial review. Some have proposed a solution to the security/liberty impasse: Appoint a special counsel with national security clearance who can view the evidence in full in order to provide a vigorous defence of a detainee in camera.

Perhaps the issues are best summarized by Michael Ignatieff, who says in his book *The Lesser Evil* that the war on terror waged since September 11, 2001, has put a strain on democracy itself, because it is mostly waged in secret, using means that are at the edge of both law and morality. He writes: "It is never justified to confine or deport an alien or citizen in secret proceedings. Openness in any process where human liberty is at stake is simply definitional of what a democracy is . . . A democracy in which most people don't vote, in which many judges accord undue deference to executive decisions, and in which government refuses adversarial review of its measures is not likely to keep the right balance between security and liberty. A war on terror is not just a challenge to democracy; it is an interrogation of the vitality of its capacity for adversarial review."2

1. On Feb. 23, 2007, the Supreme Court of Canada unanimously voted 9-0 that the security certificate system was unconstitutional. The government passed a new security law in 2008.

For details of the case see http://www.cbc.ca/canada/story/2009/08/21/f-security-certificates.html

2. In early 2009 A Federal Court judge ordered the release of the last of five foreign nationals being held on controversial national security certificates. http://www.cbc.ca/canada/toronto/story/2009/01/02/terrorism-suspect.html

The Government's Discrimination

Canada fully understands and appreciates and shares the United States' concerns with regard to security. However, the Canadian government has every right to go to bat when it believes one of its citizens has been treated unfairly by another government.
—STEPHEN HARPER, January 26, 2007

These words, spoken after settlement of the Maher Arar affair, were crafted to allay suspicions about Mr Harper's willingness to stand up to the Bush administration on matters of Canadian sovereignty. However, in view of Ottawa's defence of the gulag that is Guantanamo, and its fear of upsetting Washington by allowing Canadian citizen Abousfian Abdelrazik to return from Sudan, we can be forgiven for suspecting that our PM was indeed beholden to George W Bush.

For many immigrants to this great land, the post-9/11 era is one of insecurity, in which they wonder: What value is my Canadian passport when travelling abroad? Will my government stand up for my basic rights, or trade them to curry favour with certain regimes?

By placing politics above principles on the Omar Khadr[1] and Abdelrazik[2] files, our government has brought into question the value of citizenship, and raised the ugly spectre of discrimination against Arabs and Muslims.

Given government complicity in the rendition of Mr Arar; the apparent collusion with foreign security services in the detention and alleged torture of Abdullah Almalki, Ahmad El Maati and Muayyed Nureddin[3]; the use of secret evidence to detain immigrants (Hassan Almrei, Adil Charkaoui, Mohamed Harkat, Mahmoud Jaballah and Mohamed Zeki Mahjoub);[4] and the plights of Mr Khadr and Mr Abdelrazik, it is clear that suspicion of the "other" has played a key role in the suspension of civil liberties of Muslim and Arab men.

These examples also send a sharp message to Canadian Muslims and Arabs: "Our security agencies will cooperate with the worst of the worst if we, or the Americans, have suspicions about you. Your Canadian citizenship means nothing, and your government will let you languish in a hell-hole if need be."

Furthermore, the contrast between the government's treatment of Mr Khadr and Mr Abdelrazik with that of Brenda Martin[5] leave many wondering about the existence of two-tiered citizenship. Or, as Mr Abdelrazik explained his detention, "The Canadian government has a racist mind. It is because I am black and Muslim."[6]

Conservative supporters will counter with the federal government's stand on Huseyin Celil, a Canadian Muslim imprisoned in China. But this has more to do with the governing party's dislike of Beijing. If the Conservatives acted on principle, rather than politics, they would not distinguish among Mr Celil, Mr Khadr, and Mr Abdelrazik, and safeguard their human rights equally.

The spectre of discrimination was also raised in an open letter to Mr Harper by eminent politicians Joe Clark, Lloyd Axworthy, Flora MacDonald, Bill Graham, John Manley, and Pierre Pettigrew, who wrote: "The quest for genuine human security must be rooted in international human-rights standards: basic and hard-won standards for the just treatment of all people, everywhere, all the time and under all circumstances—no exceptions. This is especially true in times of danger and public anxiety when governments use so-called 'necessity' to justify the abuse of some people, often those who are already the targets of discrimination."[7] We should uphold these noble principles by also demanding the just treatment of Mohamed el-Attar, an Egyptian Canadian imprisoned in Egypt on espionage charges. Mr El-Attar claims he was tortured into providing a confession.

Exacerbation of racism at times of public anxiety is not new. Our history is replete with episodes of abuses in which the collective rights of identifiable groups were trampled in the name of security. During both world wars, the government interned Canadians of various ethnicities. With the operation of the War Measures Act, hundreds of innocent Quebeckers were rounded up on suspicion of indépendentiste leanings. And since the events of September 11, 2001, Muslims and Arabs have come under suspicion—especially if they oppose American or Canadian foreign policy.

By all means, let's be vigilant about our security. Yet, in a manner that is consistent with values of basic human decency. Let's not repeat the mistakes of our past, remembering that government excesses cannot be left unchallenged. Canadians of good conscience must join together to fight for the basic human dignity of their fellow citizens. With each fresh revelation about human-rights violations perpetrated in the name of security, we must heighten our vigilance against abuses of power, and demand due process for those who are detained or exiled unjustly.

1. Omar Ahmed Khadr, a Canadian citizen born in Toronto, was captured by American forces at the age of fifteen in Afghanistan and charged with war crimes and supporting terrorism. To date he has spent seven years in Guantanamo Bay, the only Western citizen remaining there. Despite urgings by various organizations, including Amnesty International, UNICEF, and the Canadian Bar Association, and rulings by the federal Court of Canada and the Court of Appeals, the Canadian government has refused demand repatriation. The Federal Court judge, in his 43-page ruling, said that the "ongoing refusal of Canada to request Mr. Khadr's repatriation to Canada offends a principle of fundamental justice and violates Mr. Khadr's rights." Canada's Conservative government has decided to appeal the decision. (See www.cbcnews.ca; http://en.wikipedia.org/wiki/Omar _Khadr).

2. Abousfian Abdelrazik, a Montrealer who was stranded in Sudan for six years because the Canadian government refused to issue him a new passport. He is suing Ottawa for $27 million.

3. see note 2 on p.51.

4. see article "Canadian Double-talk" on p.52.

5. In 2006, Brenda Martin was convicted of fraud in Mexico and sentenced to five years in jail. Her case became a cause célèbre in Canada, with government ministers involved and calls for a tourism boycott of Mexico. Martin was released and allowed to serve out her sentence in Canada. She was released on parole. (http://www.cbc.ca/canada/toronto/story/2008/12/30/ brenda-martin.html).

6. *Globe and Mail* interview, July 1, 2008.

7. Open Letter in *Globe and Mail*, Feb 1, 2007.

Outsourcing Torture:
Government Duplicity

"Shut Up and Let Me Go", the title of the 2002 Ting Tings hit, is one way to describe the behaviour of government and security agencies towards the four Canadian citizens who were imprisoned and tortured by the Syrians. That's right—four. Not just Maher Arar. But Abdullah Almalki, Ahmad El Maati and Muayyed Nureddin as well.[1]

While Canadians expressed outrage at what happened to Mr Arar, we were led to believe that this was a unique occurrence. Yet, as human-rights activist Kerry Pither reveals in her book *Dark Days: The Story of Four Canadians Tortured in the Name of Fighting Terror*, Mr Arar's year in hell was part of a larger pattern of Canada's cooperation with Syrian military intelligence in the detention and interrogation of three other Canadian citizens.

Given the secrecy enveloping the federal inquiry, led by former Supreme Court justice Frank Iacobucci, into what happened to these men, the mantle of national security is shielding the transparency and accountability of government agencies that have tremendous power to probe into our lives.

Ms Pither spent extensive time with the four men, reviewing their experiences with the Canadian Security Intelligence Service, the RCMP, and Syrian military intelligence. While Mr Arar was shipped off by the Americans, Mr Almalki, Mr El Maati and Mr Nureddin were each detained by Syrian officials during family visits. Ms Pither calls these "opportunistic renditions" facilitated by Canada.

All four were under investigation in Canada, held in the same notorious Far' Falastin prison near Damascus, interrogated by the same team of thugs, and asked questions that could have come only from Canada. They endured unspeakable violence, providing false confessions in a bid to end the torture. Yet, not one of them has been charged in Syria or in Canada.

Upon return to Canada, these four citizens suffered further indignity of a well-orchestrated smear campaign by "anonymous" officials who painted them as terrorists. Some journalists failed to question their sources' motives and, instead, allowed themselves to be used in the smearing campaign. No evidence has ever been publicly produced to back up these allegations. In contrast, as documented in *Dark Days*, there is ample evidence of wrongdoing on the part of Canadian agencies.

Piecing together the "evidence" based on public facts, Ms Pither believes that guilt by association was the chief modus operandi. The case began with the infamous Ottawa map seized from Mr El Maati's truck at the US border in August of 2001 that showed schematics of government buildings—including sites for a virus lab and atomic energy—individually numbered. As *The Globe and Mail* discovered, the map—numbers and all—was a standard (and outdated) government-issued map for courier services. The virus lab and atomic energy site had already been relocated.

Nonetheless, security officials engaged in their own game of "six degrees of separation," zealously connecting real and imaginary dots, and ensnaring anyone who fit the preconceived profile of an al-Qaeda wannabe. Acknowledging lack of evidence to convict any of their suspects, they went on to "disrupt and diffuse" the so-called threat by means that at times circumvented the law.

Men and women of conscience stood up to powerful government forces to demand justice for the voiceless. Ms Pither found her inspiration in the tenacity of hope expressed by these four men. Mr El Maati, for instance, considers himself to be one of the "lucky ones"—he made it out alive.

It is ironic that these four men have had the courage to open their lives to public scrutiny in their quest for account-ability, while those responsible for Canada's program of outsourcing torture hide behind the cowardly walls of anonymity and secrecy.

We must examine the erosion of fundamental democratic principles that has occurred in this country in the name of national security. As the Arar case illustrates, individual Canadians do have the power to make a difference in the quest for justice.

1. see notes on p.51.

Islam in the World

This Way Forward for Muslims

Crisis of the Muslim Mind; Ethics of Disagreement in Islam; The Islamic Awakening: Between Extremism and Rejectionism. These English translations of Arabic treatises are but a sampling of fundamental issues that have emerged over the past few decades as Muslim societies grapple with intellectual malaise, internecine conflict, and the dangers of extremism.

Long before September 11, 2001, Muslim scholars and activists were asking, "What's wrong with the Muslim world?" The consensus can best be summarized by the Koranic verse, "God does not change the condition of people until they change what is within themselves."

Classical Muslim scholars explained this verse to mean that God showers blessings upon people, and only changes their condition when they forget their humble beginnings, substituting gratefulness with arrogance.

Fourteen centuries later, as Muslim populations emerged from colonialism, activists returned to this verse, albeit with a different take. Wretched conditions will not change, they exhorted, until people take the initiative to change their own condition. It was, in essence, a call to recover the dynamic Islamic tenet of personal responsibility for one's actions before the Creator.

One of the classical writings on this theme was *Shikwa-Jawab-e-Shikwa* (Complaint and Answer) written in 1912 by Muhammad Iqbal, poet laureate of the Indian subcontinent. In *Shikwa*, Muslims complain to God about their miserable conditions of poverty, illiteracy, and subjugation; all the while, they pray, fast, perform hajj and recite the Koran. In

Jawab-e-Shikwa (Response to the Complaint), they are told to look in the mirror, to see how much they have fallen short in living the essential features of Islam, such as truthfulness, intelligent inquiry, and mercy. Dogmatism, hair-splitting, and hypocrisy are all condemned as attempts to replace substance with disingenuous form.

Iqbal's urgent call for reform seemed to be for naught as the Muslim world experienced two devastating losses during the 20th century: the dismantling of the Ottoman Caliphate in 1924, and the loss of Jerusalem in 1967. The former represented an institution of governance spanning fourteen centuries, while the latter represented a spiritual nexus of worship, next only to Mecca and Medina. Today, many see the 1991 war in the Persian Gulf, the brutal occupation of Palestine, genocidal sanctions against the Iraqi people, and the stationing of US troops in Saudi Arabia as further humiliations.

While some seek to blame external elements, a corps of Muslim scholars and activists look to the internal: The wretched conditions faced by Muslims will not cease until there is a fundamental change from within. If Muslims are to emerge from their chronic instability, these scholars argue, faith in God must be strengthened. Self-defeating attitudes prevalent among Muslims—reliance on conspiracy theories, blaming the West, victimization, nostalgia for a "golden age" of Islam, and the search for a saviour—all reflect weakness in faith in God. While such an approach may seem arcane to the secular mind, the importance of the Divine in Muslim thought should not be underestimated.

Contemporary Muslim scholars have urged Muslims to do away with conspiracy theories. Echoing Iqbal, they point out that such theories serve to conveniently absolve Muslims of personal responsibility to change their situation for the better. "Why bother trying when someone else controls your destiny?" is the pathetic refrain.

This outlook further places Muslims at a psychological disadvantage, for it makes one's adversaries seem more powerful than is actually true. When one knows that all power belongs to God, the fear of one's enemies diminishes. A renowned Muslim scholar based in the Middle East advises that Muslims will not solve homegrown problems of corruption, illiteracy, and sectarianism by constantly blaming the West.

Malcolm X struggled against racism by taking responsibility for his own shortcomings and finding the fortitude to face future battles, all within the moral framework of the Koran. In particular, one cannot use racism as a perpetual cover for one's own shortcomings. In today's post-9/11 climate, Muslims need to fortify from within, and then face the challenges of Islamophobia.

The Koran also encourages people to look to history to see God's moral plan. Civilizations have come and gone; their destruction being a result of their own arrogance and moral corruption. Muslims are not immune to this paradigm; the golden age of Islamic rule gradually came to an end for the same reasons as the demise of other empires. Today, some Muslims look back to that age with longing, with little analysis of what led to ascendancy, and what led to decline. Nostalgia, without a moral lesson, leads to intellectual paralysis.

Over the past few decades, Muslims have looked towards autocratic leaders as saviours to lead them out of their current dilemma. Like the Tin Man, the Scarecrow, and the Lion in *The Wizard of Oz*, they believe the only way to improve their lot is to place hope in some larger-than-life figure—an Osama bin Laden, for example. Inevitably, they are disappointed. Just as the Oz characters discover their own heart, intelligence, and courage, Muslims, too, need to uncover their own potential.

With the failure of pan-Arabism and communism, and the current antipathy toward the United States, Muslim populations are turning to Islam as the indigenous solution. The future struggle will lie in how it is interpreted and implemented.

Why Muslims Are Angry

"A History of Terrorism," the title of a 2003 exhibit at Harvard's Lamont Library, provided much food for thought. Probing the maxim "one man's terrorist is another man's freedom fighter," it asked viewers to consider why relatively small-scale terrorist attacks were strongly condemned, while acts such as the Second World War firebombing of Dresden and the use of the atomic bomb against Hiroshima and Nagasaki were often considered justified.

It also revealed a strategy for future American foreign policy, based on a declassified 1948 document that was premised on the fact that the United States had half the world's wealth and only 6.3 percent of its population. "We cannot fail to be the object of envy and resentment," the document read. "Our real task in the coming period is to devise a pattern of relationships that will permit us to maintain this position of disparity without positive detriment to our nation's security."

Given the growth in that disparity since 1948, this strategy is key to understanding American foreign policy during the past half a century.

Among Muslim nations, the invasion of Iraq is seen in this

light as the first step toward increased American hegemony in the region, fuelled, Muslims believe, by the motive of controlling oil supply. There is further concern that American policy—both domestic and international—has religious overtones.

Since 9/11, Muslims worldwide have heard influential American Christian evangelical leaders demean Islam and the Prophet Muhammad, especially during the Bush presidency. Analysts attributed the silence to the Republican Party's need to secure the "religious right." Indeed, after the 2002 electoral victory, the White House issued a public rebuke against religious anti-Islamic diatribe to show Muslims that the United States was not at war with Islam.

But Muslims are also keenly aware of the security crackdown in the US that has targeted their community with secret detentions, summary deportations and the profiling of nationals from predominately Muslim countries.

They have also seen the death of thousands of fellow Muslims in the aftermath of the American bombardment of Afghanistan, along with the imposition of a US-backed leader for the maintenance of American interests in the region—namely, regional security and the construction of an oil pipeline through the impoverished nation.

And, for the past sixty years, Muslims have witnessed the brutal occupation of the Palestinian homeland by successive Israeli governments, with full military and financial backing by Washington.

Many see double standards in the American justification for war on Iraq. If the goal is disarmament, what about North Korea, a nation with far more dangerous capabilities? If it is the flouting of United Nations resolutions, what about Israel, which has ignored some sixty-four resolutions (and counting) with American approval?

The latest American case for war is to spread democracy.

There is no doubt the people of the Middle East would welcome democracy, but most have been denied it by regimes, many of which are backed by the US. And the people know their exercise of democracy is acceptable to Washington only as long as the people's choice agrees with that of Uncle Sam—remember Algeria's 1991 election when Washington supported military intervention after an Islamic party was poised to take office?

Muslims' distrust of American intentions is strengthened when they learn that strategies for extending American influence in the Persian Gulf were in the works well before 9/11. A paper prepared by the neo-conservative think-tank Project for the New American Century for the incoming Bush administration stated: "The United States has for decades sought to play a more permanent role in Gulf regional security. While the unresolved conflict with Iraq provides the immediate justification, the need for substantial American force presence in the Gulf transcends the issue of the regime of Saddam Hussein."

There has been widespread sentiment in the Muslim world that the war in Iraq was undertaken for the strengthening of Israel, as part of George W Bush's plan to remake the Middle East. *The New Yorker* reported on a policy paper circling amongst US hawks, called "A Clean Break: A New Strategy for Securing the Realm," written in 1996 by US foreign policy analysts as advice for then Israeli prime minister Benjamin Netanyahu. The title refers to a foreign policy for Israel that would de-emphasize the peace process between Israelis and Palestinians and move "to a traditional concept of strategy based on balance of power." One key item in the strategy, the paper implies, would be toppling Saddam Hussein.

But the real heart of the anger felt by Muslims is the violence that has been meted out to the Iraqi people. The equating of Islam with violence by Western pundits is seen as the pinnacle of hypocrisy when you consider that 90,000 tons of bombs—the equivalent of 7½ Hiroshima bombs—were dropped on the people of Iraq in the 43 days of the 1991 gulf war, and that UN sanctions contributed to the death of hundreds of thousands of Iraqis afterward.

With the occupation of Iraq, Muslims worldwide were reminded of the consequences the last time a superpower invaded and occupied Muslim land: the Soviet Union's 1979 invasion of Afghanistan. After thirteen years of bitter fighting and one million Afghan dead, the occupiers left when the cost became too high for them.

Many have viewed the war on Iraq as a war against Islam. In the fall of 2002, a group of more than 200 prominent Muslims accused the United States of leading a crusade against Islam and warned that an assault on Iraq could provoke revenge attacks against Western targets.

"There is a feeling that we are powerless," said Tariq Ramadan, the highly respected Swiss-based Islamic scholar who has written extensively on finding common ground between Muslims and the West. "We can't speak about a 'clash of civilizations' yet, but the ingredients are there and, after an attack on Iraq, they will be stronger."

Love-Hate

While attending a wedding in Lahore, Pakistan, a while back, I got into a heated discussion with a cousin about the dysfunction of so many Muslim countries. I pointed to Lahore's Gadhafi Stadium as an example of our skewed moral compass. "How can Pakistan name a stadium after someone who has wreaked so much havoc on so many?" My cousin

replied with emotion, "Moammar Gadhafi came for an offi-
cial visit. We honoured him. He's done a lot for his people.
Besides, he is the only Muslim leader who stands up to the
United States! In our eyes, he is a hero."

My cousin was a medical student, not particularly religious. I couldn't reconcile his anger towards America on one
hand, with his effusive appreciation for the Harvard medical
school polo shirt I had brought him as a gift—he hated
America, yet loved her schools.

This love-hate relationship is being taken seriously by the
American government. On October 1, 2003, Congress
unveiled an eighty-five-page report, "Changing Minds,
Winning Peace"—the culmination of a five-month study of
opinions in the Muslim world. An earlier poll by the Pew
Center for Research had shown that "the bottom has fallen
out of Arab and Muslim support for the United States." The
inquiry aimed to find out why, what to do about it, and how
to marginalize the appeal of extremists.

Muslims in the Middle East, North Africa, Europe,
Pakistan, and Indonesia expressed a desire for social justice, a
fair judiciary, honest multiparty elections, and freedom of the
press, of religion and of expression. They admired American
entrepreneurship, its democratic and educational institutions, and its adherence to the rule of law. If these results seem
surprising, that's only because of our media's focus on
extremist rhetoric and actions of autocratic governments—
neither of which represents the wider aspirations of Muslims.

The report marked the first time a genuine effort has been
made by the West to listen to the public mood: "We have
failed to listen and failed to persuade . . . We have not both-
ered to help them understand us," states the report. The world
can no longer afford such miscommunication.

Why the anger against America? Muslims are angry at
Washington's support of Israel at the expense of the

Palestinians; the bombardment of Afghanistan; and a decade of war, sanctions, and occupation of Iraq. Disappointingly, however, the congressional report advises no change—not even reflection on change—in foreign policy.

American support of undemocratic regimes in the Arab and Muslim world prompts many to believe that the US wants freedom and democracy only for itself. And the report acknowledges that America is ambivalent about democracy if it benefits (i.e. elects) extremists. But this attitude implies that Muslims cannot be trusted to choose their form of government, while justifying outside intervention in the internal affairs of sovereign nations. It also hints that the only acceptable democracy is one with an American hue.

Most of the report recommends ways to counteract anti-American propaganda spewed by extremists. The goal—to educate Muslims about true American values, thereby "changing minds, winning peace"—is laudable. But Muslims know too well the disconnect between American ideals and American actions abroad. Reinforcing the former without rectifying the latter can have the unintended effect of sharpening this contradiction—playing into the hands of Osama bin Laden. We in the West, attuned only to his violence, are oblivious to the remainder of his message that speaks forcefully to the pent-up anger felt by Muslims about US interference in their affairs.

Consider the startling 2003 Pew survey result: Significant populations in Indonesia (58 percent), Jordan (55 percent), Morocco (49 percent), Pakistan (45 percent) and the Palestinian National Authority (71 percent) expressed confidence in Mr bin Laden to "do the right thing regarding world affairs." Some may dismiss this as a Robin Hood phenomenon—the cheering of an outlaw who tweaks the hegemon's nose. But it is worrisome to see the moral compass skewed again, pointing to Mr Gadhafi yesterday, Mr bin Laden today.

The most puzzling aspect of the congressional report is its abrupt dismissal of the popular opinion "We like Americans but not what the Americans are doing." The report's authors state, "This distinction is unrealistic, since Americans elect their government and broadly support its foreign policy." But most Americans elect their governments for domestic reasons; they're ignorant of US foreign policy and its effect on the lives of non-Americans.

All of this is relevant to Canadians because a Commons committee is completing a similar study. Canada's peacekeeping efforts and international developmental projects have earned respect abroad, as has our stand against the invasion of Iraq. We are in an excellent position to help bridge the Muslim-American divide. Do we take this responsibility seriously?

Islamic Financing

Islamic financing is the latest target of self-declared vanguards against so-called sharia creep, who warn that sharia-compliant financial products are tools to sneak Islamic law through the back door into countries like Canada. This drumbeat of fear was used during the debate over faith-based arbitration in Ontario. The shrill language reduced the issue to: "You're either with us or with the Islamists." The furor obscured any pragmatic approach to the use of Islamic principles by Canadian Muslims in settling family disputes.

Muslim reliance on faith-based principles can also extend to personal finance. In 2008, *The New York Times* reported that about 300 Islamic financial institutions around the world held a total of more than $500-billion in assets, an amount increasing by about 10 percent a year. The biggest Islamic banks are in the Gulf states, but there are untapped markets in Turkey, North Africa, Indonesia, and Europe.

The topic is also being explored by academics. In 1998, Harvard Business School published a landmark study on Islamic law and finance in conjunction with Harvard Law School's Islamic legal studies department. Soon after, Harvard's Islamic Finance Project took flight.

The Koran clearly prohibits usury, as do the Torah and the Bible. Aristotle denounced it, while the early Christian church prohibited charging high interest rates to lend money, as the *Times* noted. Western theologians eventually distinguished interest from usury, and reintroduced it during the Renaissance.

In Islamic financing, the financier is required to share the borrower's risk. Deals are akin to lease-to-own arrangements, layaway plans, joint purchase-and-sale agreements, or partnerships. Proponents say risk-sharing reduces the types of abuses that were at the heart of the subprime mortgage fiasco of 2008.

It's possible to purchase a home this way, without engaging in a conventional interest-based mortgage. In 1975, the first Canadian Islamic home-financing agreement was drafted in Halifax. A group of Muslims pooled their money to buy a home, which was rented at market value to a buyer-tenant. All owners paid maintenance costs and taxes, received rental income and owned shares in the house.

After a year, the house price and rent were reappraised. The buyer-tenant obtained a little more home equity by buying back shares from the other owners. She paid rent, but received a portion thereof as a co-owner. With increasing home equity, her monthly payments were reduced each year until she owned all the shares.

The arrangement was flexible—payments could be accelerated, allowing outright home ownership in a shorter period of time, or slowed, in case of financial difficulties. The investors and the buyer shared in the home's gain or loss in value. The first purchase spanned a period of three years, and the total amount paid for the house was less than it would have been with a conventional mortgage.

Toronto-based Ansar Co-operative Housing Corporation uses a variant of this model. Since 1981, it has sold 700 homes across the country, with a near 100 percent success rate. Ansar's chair, Pervez Nasim, believes that maximizing profit is not the most important aspect of the business. "Charity and social responsibility are part and parcel with the bottom line," he says. When one of the co-op's customers died in a car accident, fees were waived for four months to allow his widow to grieve.

There are wrinkles. Ansar requires customers to provide a 20 percent down payment, making the service unaffordable for many first-time home buyers. One solution would be to transfer from a conventional mortgage to the co-op once 20 percent of home ownership is achieved. Another drawback is that Ansar currently offers its services to Muslims only. When the *Ottawa Citizen* ran a story on Ansar in 2002, the co-op was inundated by queries from many non-Muslim Canadians, who were turned away.

As the number of Canadian Islamic financing institutions grows in response to demand, greater regulation will be needed. In addition, the Canadian Mortgage and Housing Corporation has commissioned a study on the practice, as part of its mandate to understand all aspects of the country's housing system. For this, it was pilloried for facilitating sharia creep.

In the spring of 2008, *The Globe and Mail* reported that housing affordability across Canada was at its lowest level since 1990. In Vancouver, renting is more affordable than owning a home. Doesn't it make sense to explore alternative means of home financing? Why not an Islamic financing model, available to all Canadians?

Neighbourly Love and Mideast Debate

As the raw feelings of pain, fear, and hate spill over from the Israeli-Palestinian conflict to Jewish and Arab/Muslim communities in Canada, I cannot help but remember our Montreal neighbours of nineteen years, Sally and Bob Venor. Sally passed away in 1995; Bob, one year later.

We had moved into the house next to the Venors in NDG, a middle-class, ethnically diverse neighbourhood of Montreal. We were Muslims of Indo-Pakistani origin; they were Jewish. While our political views on the Middle East differed, it was the guiding principles of Islam and Judaism that defined our relationship. The monotheistic essence of both doctrines provided a spiritual bond. The importance of honouring one's neighbour provided the basis of a relationship based on love, dignity, and respect.

I still remember Sally, a woman of boundless optimism and generosity, telling us how she would include our family in her Friday Sabbath prayers. She was a devout woman who prayed often, and educated us about Jewish rites. She would bake cakes and send them over; take us out to lunch to Ben Ash; and always tell us how proud she was of us. And even more significant, she would say: "Palestinians are people like everyone else. They deserve to be treated fairly." She mentioned that her friends would often chastise her for such views. But she did not care. Her love for humanity extended to all.

As a deeply spiritual woman, she was one of the few who

supported my personal renewed commitment to Islam. During the completion of my PhD in chemical physics at Harvard, I underwent personal changes that reflected spiritual evolution from within. This included a change in lifestyle, wherein prayer, modesty, and gratefulness filled a void. I chose to wear the Islamic headscarf, to the consternation of my friends and family. Yet, there was Sally, fully supportive of the spiritual choice I had made. Our bond was irrevocably strengthened.

We also shared the recognition that minorities were vulnerable to prejudice. I had been involved in combating media stereotypes against Muslims, when news broke of the murder of four Concordia University professors by one of their own, Valerie Fabrikant, who happened to be Jewish. Sally was so distraught, worried that people would make wrongful generalizations about Jews. "Do you also worry about that?" she asked.

"Yes, I do," I replied, "but I will not let the media define who I am. Our community is young, and many people do not know Muslims as individuals, or our values. Besides, I am sure most people will not draw conclusions about Jews from this tragedy, because your community is such an integral part of our society. The bigots will, but they always look for something. And I know you personally; the thought never crossed my mind that the two of you had anything in common."

Sally died a few days before my wedding. I had eagerly looked forward to having her attend my big day. I wanted her to be at the mosque to witness the simplicity of an Islamic wedding contract. And I wanted her to be part of the celebration the following day. She was just like family.

Instead, I cried many tears at her funeral, saddened by her departure, yet grateful for her friendship. I worried for Bob, her husband, for the two had been inseparable. He, too, had been a wonderful neighbour, ready to offer help at a moment's notice. He was quieter than Sally, and a man of generous deeds. One year later, I wept at his funeral.

Sally and Bob come to my mind now more than ever, because they embodied hope at times of tension. They were supporters of Israel. But that did not make them anti-Palestinian. And I supported the Palestinian cause, without being anti-Jewish or anti-Israeli. Even during times of upheaval overseas—the invasion of Lebanon, the massacres at Sabra and Shatilla, the first intifada—we maintained our unique relationship. Sadly, the current rhetoric, in its efforts to dehumanize "the other" through bitter words, takes away from the tremendous human potential that exists right here in Canada to make a difference for the better.

Islamic Democracy?

Some in the West say Islam and democracy cannot coexist. Some Muslims feel the same way. But people like Osama bin Laden don't offer alternate visions of governance; they're not interested in building states, but destroying them. Meanwhile, hundreds of years of Islamic culture say that democracy and Islam are compatible—provided democracy is rooted in Islamic values.

Developing such a democracy is also the vision of Noah Feldman, a New York University law professor and author of *After Jihad: America and the Struggle for Islamic Democracy*, and an adviser appointed by the Bush administration to help set up the interim Iraqi governing council. Professor Feldman points out that Judaism and democracy coexist in the state of Israel; true, there are tensions, but they are creative tensions.

Muslim scholars and intellectuals of diverse backgrounds

agree that Islam emphasizes certain fundamentals of governance—justice, human dignity and equality, the rule of law, the role of people in selecting their leaders, the obligation of consultative government, and the value of pluralism. Clearly, these elements are lacking in many Muslim countries. But a sweeping new international poll shows that a majority of Muslims believe that their political institutions must become more democratic, even as they find a greater role for religious leaders.

In 2003, the Pew Research Center for the People and the Press surveyed the political, social, and religious attitudes of Muslims in fourteen countries—Mali, Indonesia, Pakistan, Turkey, Bangladesh, Lebanon, Jordan, Uzbekistan, Nigeria, Ghana, Uganda, Tanzania, Senegal, and the Ivory Coast. Interestingly, the Egyptian government did not permit survey questions pertaining to democracy.

The survey found that a majority of Muslims in nine countries wanted Islam to play a large role in politics, while a slim majority favoured the opposite in Lebanon, Turkey, Senegal, and Uzbekistan.

In countries where Muslims support a greater role for Islam in politics, people also told pollsters that they valued freedom of speech, freedom of the press, and free elections. Majorities also placed high importance on the freedom to openly criticize the government, judicial systems that treat everyone the same, and honest multiparty electoral systems—ideals that are in harmony with Islamic values. (Jordan, a monarchy with a limited parliament, was an exception; less than one-third expressed support for such freedoms.)

When asked what kind of leadership they would trust, most of those surveyed preferred a democratic government to a strong autocratic leader (the exceptions were Jordan, Uzbekistan, and Nigeria). The Uzbekistan view that a strong central authority is the best form of governance was in line with other post-Soviet-bloc nations (such as Russia and Ukraine).

But for those who favoured democracy, the question remains: What kind of democracy? The Pew pollsters didn't probe the particulars, but did ask Muslims what they thought of American-style democracy. The result: Solid majorities in Turkey, Indonesia, Pakistan, and Jordan expressed dislike.

That's not a contradiction, even if some American observers interpret it that way. The fact is, democracy comes in many forms. But the practical question remains: How can Muslims combine democratic ideals with their faith?

In secular democracies that strictly separate church and state, this may seem impossible. But if you look back at Islamic governance over fourteen centuries, you find a system akin to constitutional democracy serving as the foundation of certain states. The norms of the Koran and the sunnah (the authentic traditions of the Prophet Muhammad) served as the constitution, while bodies of independent scholars provided rulings in light of these texts.

The principle of public participation was enshrined by the institution of shurah (consultation), but such consultation could not contradict the constitution. Moreover, the constitution required that the laws be applied equally to both the ruling class and the ruled. On occasion, the ruler would disregard the scholars' rulings; at times, courageous scholars would choose prison over bending to tyranny.

Canadians should recognize aspects of such a democracy. We have a constitutional democracy, in that the democratic will (represented by Parliament) is subject to the Constitution as interpreted by the courts, whose rulings are binding on the government (which may opt out by invoking the notwithstanding clause, but even that exceptional step is enshrined in the Constitution).

Today, it's a challenge to find one Muslim nation that abides by an Islamic model of constitutional democracy. Most are dysfunctional, with power concentrated in the hands of a few, little accountability of government leaders, and no checks and balances to set things right.

And here's another problem turned up by the Pew poll: while Muslims favour democratic elements in political life, Muslim majorities in ten of the nations surveyed rejected the idea that Islam should tolerate diverse interpretations. Yet the view that there should be only one true interpretation of Islam is supported neither by authentic Islamic texts, nor by history. The concept of hajj (pilgrimage to Mecca) has made the Muslim community something of a global village. Writing seven centuries ago, the Moroccan traveller Ibn Battuta described the richness of thought in the Islamic empire that he saw in his travels from North Africa to China. The fact that at least five major schools of Islamic jurisprudence have evolved is yet another sign of the diversity of interpretation.

The survey result regarding interpretation is thus all the more perplexing. Does it mean that Muslims are looking for a central body of qualified scholars to provide one uniform interpretation of the religion? Whose interpretation would be taken as "true"?

Islamic thought has sustained and nourished a rich world of scholarly opinion over the centuries. Muslims today must remember that.

Fearing Dubai

Sipping a latte at Café Havana, atop a mall for the well-heeled (is there any other kind?) in Dubai, I peer down at the multitudes below. It seems every single nationality on the planet is represented here. Dubai has to be the most cosmopolitan city in the world. Men in long, flowing white abayas, crowned with elegant headdresses, walk alongside Armani-clad movers and shakers. Chanel clients nonchalantly peruse diamonds alongside women fully covered from head to toe. Perhaps those black robes conceal the latest from Fendi.

The next morning, the chi-chi mall experience seems a distant memory. I visit a mosque where a class for memorizing the Koran is under way. However, unlike any mosque I know of in Canada, this space is off-limits to men each morning. Women of all ages and nationalities attend, following the centuries-old path of committing the Koran to memory. The sheika (female sheik) listens to each student attentively, pausing to gently correct for mistakes.

Dubai is a mixture of the old and the new. It combines the business acumen of Hong Kong, the discipline of Singapore, and the best of Arab hospitality. This city-state is open to the world, and the world has come flocking. Canadians fearful of immigrants with "strange" attire and values should note that immigrants form 85 percent of Dubai's population. New arrivals need not wear indigenous attire (abayas or chadors), nor are they screened for their values. Yet, as the Dubai Ports World controversy in the United States in 2006 showed, few in the West know much about this Gulf powerhouse.

Oil was found in Dubai in the 1970s. Since reserves were set to dwindle within thirty years or so, the ruling Maktoum family set forth an ambitious diversification plan to reinvest oil profits for the benefit of the state. Many credit the liberal, outward-looking and progressive policies of the late Sheik Maktoum bin Rashid al Maktoum for the emergence of Dubai as a cosmopolitan financial hub. Dubai has plans to diversify its economy into three areas: oil and gas (5 percent), tourism (70 percent) and knowledge (25 percent).

Dubai's leaders were acutely aware of the bleak educational prospects in the Middle East well before the dismal 2003 UN Arab Human Development Report. And so their visionary response reaches beyond reversing the brain drain and revamping the region's education system. Dubai intends to become an international centre of academic excellence. The key is to focus on human capital as a means of sustaining the region's growth. The infrastructure will be provided by "free zones" devoted exclusively to sectors of the knowledge economy. "Knowledge Village," for example, will host a variety of vocational schools, along with campuses of local and international universities. In early 2006, the University of New Brunswick became the first Canadian university to establish a presence in Dubai. But perhaps one of the most ambitious projects is Dubiotech—a vast technology park devoted to research in the biotechnology, pharmaceutical, and life sciences sectors. I met with Dr Abdulqader al Khayat, executive director of Dubiotech, who is intent on attracting major players. In the spring of 2006, I learnt, three of the top five global biotech companies were expected to announce their entry into Dubiotech. IBM had agreed to provide supercomputing facilities, to open avenues into the next hot sector: nanotechnology.

This is a confident society, buoyed by hard work, discipline, and dreams. Nonetheless, the collapse of the Dubai Ports deal has left a bitter aftertaste. There is no doubt, in the minds of many here, that the issue was driven by racism.

"Other foreign-owned companies run US ports—but they were not Arab. That is the message. And we got it," said a *Gulf News* editorial. Even General John Abizaid, the top US commander in the Middle East, criticized opposition to the Dubai Ports deal, calling it "Arab and Muslim bashing." American lawmakers pandered to domestic fears while shoring up security credentials in preparation for the November 2006 mid-term elections. "Retaliation precipitated by Congress will not only harm US employers but employees as well," warned the US Chamber of Congress, adding that the imbroglio did nothing for confidence in the US economy.

The deal's collapse also has the potential to seriously affect future trade between the US and the Gulf states. A poll by *Gulf News* revealed that 64 percent of its readers had a worse opinion of investing in America. Free-trade talks between the US and the United Arab Emirates were postponed. Concerned about an economic fallout, a group of businessmen in the UAE planned to bring Oprah to Dubai, in order to educate American viewers what this region is all about.

Soon those same American lawmakers were scrambling at damage control. Four GOP congressmen visited Dubai, reiterating that the UAE remained one of America's strongest allies in the fight against terrorism. Dubai serviced more US military ships than any country in the world. "This country is not part of the problem, rather it is part of the solution," asserted Congressman Phil Gingrey. Long term, it seems the US has more to lose. In a prescient editorial prior to the Dubai Ports fiasco, the *Khaleej Times* noted that the growing economies of China and India, for example, were only too willing to welcome investments from the Gulf region. A shift in economic focus in Gulf investments from the West to the East "could have important political and economic implications in the years to come."

Using the Lessons of Canada
to Heal the Wounds of Mumbai

I was born in Varanasi, India, moved to Calcutta soon after. When I was three, my parents decided to leave Hindu-Muslim strife behind for the peaceful climes of Canada. In Montreal I grew up with my best friend Tina, a Hindu, whose family was like, well, family. Our modest apartment served as a temporary home for many of my father's friends who had come to look for work and a better life for their families. Hindu, Sikh, Parsi, Sunni, Shia—all were welcome. On weekends, we would visit other immigrant families. We all shared a sense of cultural heritage and the challenges of adapting to a new environment.

The one thing that I remember most clearly was the absence of politics. Our parents had made a conscious choice to leave strife behind and build life anew. There were definitely times of tension: the Indo-Pakistani wars, the Air-India bombing, the assassination of Indira Gandhi. Yet the key lesson was never to allow the tensions "over there" to spill over here.

Canadians from South Asia have become an integral part of the national fabric. They have seen first-hand the benefits of living in a country where there is peace. Challenges do exist. Discrimination is still out there. Yet there is a belief that hard work pays off, and that one can strive to change things for the better. The Canadian approach to multiculturalism has been embraced as a means to be part of a nation whose Charter insists on inclusiveness.

The vision of inclusiveness has permeated the South Asian

community, and it is a key to addressing violent events overseas. The horrific Mumbai attacks of 2008 were but the latest in a series of terrorist attacks perpetrated by both Hindus and Muslims. India is a complex land, with the potential for even more serious conflict. This is why the South Asian diaspora must not only condemn such violence but also work together within itself to reinforce our tolerant society. The work starts here at home, with mosques, temples, synagogues, and other houses of worship opening their doors for prayers for all those killed and injured. Organizations need to bring together diverse members of the South Asian community, along with members of the Jewish community (whose members were targeted in Mumbai) in a show of solidarity and condemn the violence. This is also the time for a collective relief effort, without questions of religion or ethnicity.

Once the shock has diminished and more information about the attacks is forthcoming, there will need to be a calm, multi-pronged approach to understanding and addressing the many complexities of the region, at a very basic human level.

The South Asian diaspora has benefited greatly from the many opportunities afforded by Canada, and in turn has contributed towards Canada's enrichment as a nation. It can now help to defuse conflicts abroad through its intimate knowledge of and familiarity with many regions of the world, its strength of resources, diversity, and desire for peace.

When my father died a few years ago, many of his long-time friends came to his funeral. They had forged friendships in India that were strengthened here in Canada. Hindu, Muslim, Sikh—they were weeping for the loss of a dear friend. We were all family.

After the events in Mumbai, let us renew the ties of humanity that bind, remembering that despair and hatred are the exact goals of the perpetrators of violence. Hope, solidarity and the resolve to build a better future—both here and in South Asia—should be our legacy.

Funny

I could never quite understand why Edmonton Oiler's coach Glen Sather put Dave Semenko on the same line as Wayne Gretzky. Semenko was a huge, bruising forward. Then Don Cherry explained it with clarity during an episode of *Coach's Corner*: mess around with Gretzky, and Semenko would make you pay. Deterrence through physical intimidation. Or in kinder, gentler terms: keeping the opposition honest.

As the cartoon fiasco of 2006 raged, some Muslims opted for a similar strategy: mess with the Prophet, and we will make you pay. We will boycott your goods and recall our ambassadors. Others chose far more violent responses. Flags were burned, embassies destroyed, calls for death and destruction shouted in the heart of Europe. It may not be pretty, many argued, but it works. The West will dare not go there again.

But something is terribly wrong with this picture. What happened to the actual example of the Prophet? Must the response be "by any means necessary?" Are we Muslims reduced to such superficial piety that we discard the very teachings of the man whose honour we are trying to defend? There is, no doubt, heartfelt anger against the editors of the Danish newspaper who published the denigrating cartoons of the Prophet as an act of provocation. Defiant republication in other countries only added fuel to the fire.

How to deal with this genuine anger? The strong man is not the one with physical prowess, cautioned Muhammad, but the one who controls oneself when angry. He advised his followers to make ritual ablutions as a means to dissipate anger. It is high time for Muslims who are still outraged to make ablution. And, one may add, time for freedom-of-expression absolutists to take a Valium.

The majority of the world's Muslims have a strong emotional attachment to the Prophet. Yet, how much does this majority know about his actual life? His magnanimous examples of forgiveness and mercy in the face of insults. His humility before God. His compassion for all people. It is fair to say that the protracted cartoon outrage was a testimony to widespread ignorance about his life. Not to mention basic Islamic precepts regarding proportional response to affronts.

Take, for example, the burning of flags. For a secular West, this action represents anger toward Denmark. From an Islamic perspective, the flag is both a Christian symbol (the cross) and an emblem of identity for the Danes. The Koran emphatically prohibits its desecration. How then could Muslims brazenly burn Danish flags in front of cameras—especially after attending Friday prayers?

Hopefully, this incident will serve as a catalyst for Muslims themselves to study the life of the Prophet in greater detail. To see how far we have strayed from his path. And to see how his call is so antithetical to that of Osama bin Laden and Abu Musab al-Zarqawi. Too many Muslims view contemporary events through the prism of anti-Western rhetoric, rather than the light of the Prophet's example.

Yes, there are legitimate grievances. But the response must be rooted in prophetic traditions—not misguided demagoguery.

During the first Gulf war, Saddam Hussein held a vulgar spectacle of displaying Western hostages trapped in Baghdad. Verbal declarations of piety were broadcast to shore up his Muslim credentials. I knew that Saddam was playing the religion card. But I was curious to know how the Prophet dealt with prisoners of war. During his time, prisoners were treated humanely, with dignity. Relatives would pay for their release. Those who did not have such means, could win their freedom by teaching ten children how to read. Imagine—bartering literacy for freedom. Shouldn't this be somewhere in the Geneva Conventions?

As one delves into his life, one cannot help but see a grand vision for humanity at large. It is not the us-versus-them mentality espoused by extremists on both sides of the divide. Sadly, it is this small group that is driving the cycle of misunderstanding and conflict.

In North America, Edward Luttwak denigrates Islam. A *Globe and Mail* editorial heaps disdain on all Islamic societies, while praising Bernard Lewis—a British scholar who, according to Brent Scowcroft, once advised the Bush White House: "I believe that one of the things you've got to do to Arabs is hit them between the eyes with a big stick. They respect power."[1]

A few obscure Canadian publications chose to publish the offensive cartoons—oblivious to the potentially deadly consequences for our troops in Afghanistan. Our well-intentioned goal of helping Afghans rebuild civil society might well have been sabotaged by the actions of a few.

We must work hard to ensure that this does not happen. Just as we must make sure that the actions of extremists in the Muslim world do not sabotage the on-going project of inter-cultural dialogue.

It has been heartening to see that the majority have reacted responsibly. Freedoms have been weighed carefully against responsibilities. Anger has been channelled into education, dialogue, and, one would hope, forgiveness for those who provocatively insult. Our common values encourage dialogue, hope, and respect.

Some time ago, my son made a beautiful three-dimensional Islamic calligraphy design using Lego. He loves Lego, a Danish toy that unleashes the creative imagination in children (and adults) of all ages. He is also proud of who he is. He combined the two in an artistic expression of his identity, with the pure simple intention of a child. That sparked the following idea.

Instead of boycotting Danish food products, here is a challenge to Muslim communities across Canada. Buy Lego for your kids. Let them use it to build their own masterpieces from their rich Islamic heritage. An observatory. A hospital. A mosque. For Canadian content, throw in some Mega-Bloks. Let's encourage them to see a world of possibilities, not a world of conflict.

1. *New Yorker*, October 31, 2008. "Bucking Ranks" by Jeffrey Goldberg.

The Soul in Science

In November 2002, while the world's attention was focused on Iraq, thieves stole a rare first edition of Isaac Newton's *Philosophiae Naturalis Principia Mathematica* from the Russian National Library in St Petersburg. A few weeks later, police announced its recovery to an uninterested world. *Principia*, first published in 1687, is a key work in modern science. In it, Newton proposed the three laws of motion and the law of universal gravitation, foundations of the physical sciences and engineering.

Less well-known is *Principia*'s final chapter, in which Newton expounded on his religious beliefs: "This most beautiful system of the sun, planets and comets could only proceed from the counsel and dominion of an intelligent and powerful Being, . . . eternal and infinite, omnipotent and omniscient. . . He governs all things, and knows all things that are, or can be done. . . We adore Him as His servants."

While Newton's science propagated through time and space, his harmonization of faith and scientific inquiry did not. Instead, battles between Newton's persecuted contemporaries and the Roman Catholic Church left an indelible mark on Western thought, causing a dichotomy between science and faith that prevails today.

Reconciling the two has never been an issue in Islamic thought. The Koran invites contemplation of the natural world, pointing to signs of a wise Creator. Nothing is left to fuzzy uncertainty. As Albert Einstein said, "God does not play dice with the universe." The study of the world is a means to attain faith, as exemplified by the Prophet Abraham.

As a boy, Abraham observed the rising and setting of a star, the moon and finally the sun, each object more dazzling than its predecessor. He realized, like Newton, that however awe-inspiring, each object had no inherent power but was subject to a far greater power. Empirical research and deductive reasoning paved his way towards belief in God. He also understood that it was useless to worship objects created through human agency, inanimate creations that could not respond to the innate spiritual calling of the heart. Some would argue that the West's infatuation with technical achievements is akin to the idol worship of Abraham's time.

The exhortation towards God-consciousness impelled the nascent Islamic empire to learn from other civilizations, and to collect and translate works of the Greeks, Persians, and Chinese. For a thousand years, Muslims reviewed and refined prior thought, and—remaining within the guidelines of Islamic principles—established new frontiers in medicine, mathematics, astronomy, and geography. The Muslim world was filled with universities, observatories, and hospitals, while Europe remained in the Dark Ages. Within Islam's moral framework, ethics and social responsibility intertwined with scientific inquiry.

As the empire waned, scientific progress shifted to the West. Today, Muslim countries are home to 1.6 billion people and three-quarters of the world's fuel reserves. Yet their combined GNP is less than half that of Germany; illiteracy levels are among the world's highest; and science spending is a meager 0.2 percent of GNP. At a spring 2003 meeting of research ministers and academics in Trieste, delegates searched for the reasons. Some blamed governments that spent on arms rather than education. Others warned of excessive dogma. Yet others cited the lack of free expression and creative thinking in authoritarian regimes.

Yet in environments that prize hard work and ingenuity, Muslim scientists thrive. It's no surprise that a Muslim woman, Dr Tyseer Aboulnasr, is dean of engineering at the University of Ottawa, or that Egyptian-born Ahmed Zewail, now of Stanford University, won the 1999 Nobel Prize in Chemistry.

London-based intellectual Ziauddin Sardar has formulated a paradigm of Islamic science in which God-consciousness leads to accountability for one's scientific activities. The scientist strives to use knowledge to promote social justice and public interest, and to avoid pursuits that lead to one's own destruction and that of the environment.

Such a model has implications for emerging technologies such as stem-cell research. Pending Canadian legislation forbids the creation of embryos expressly for research purposes. Only extra embryos discarded at fertility clinics can be used. The couple involved must give full consent; and no money can be exchanged for the creation or use of the embryos. The embryo can develop for a maximum of fourteen days before use.

Islamic scholars issued an almost identical ruling one year earlier, based on Islamic jurisprudence and consultation with leading scientists. The additional requirement of marriage between the couple safeguards the family unit, while a two to three-day limit for embryo development has roots in theological texts.

This example suggests further exploration of common ground. The West can assist with technological transfer to Muslim countries; Muslim scientists can in turn help foster a holistic paradigm in which social responsibility and ethics are integrated into science policy. Perhaps scientists can work towards a much-needed symbiosis, rather than clash, of civilizations.

The Canadian Way

I Was a Teenage Hijabi Hockey Player

"When I used to play hockey," I began telling my co-workers over lunch. All of a sudden, eyes looked up in disbelief. "You played hockey?" asked a friend incredulously. "Yes," I replied with a smile, thinking, "Doesn't every Canadian play hockey at some point in their life?" And then it hit me. Muslim women, especially hijabis, aren't expected to be interested in sports, let alone play. Perhaps a calming sport like croquet. But hockey?

Come on! I grew up cheering the Montreal Canadiens. My allegiance to the Habs was minted during their phenomenal upset Stanley Cup win in 1971 that featured a law student/goalie named Ken Dryden (I still have his rookie card). My love of the game reached its zenith during that magical September of 1972. I still remember cheering passionately with the rest of my school when Paul Henderson scored in Game 8.

During the '70s, I, like many Montrealers, became spoiled by the Canadiens. Every May, my friends and I would line up on Ste-Catherine Street to see the "annual" Stanley Cup parade. One year, we lingered near City Hall, and were rewarded with meeting Bob Gainey, Yvan Cournoyer, and Ken Dryden. My seven-year-old brother refused to wash his hands for days.

I grew up playing street hockey, driveway hockey and table hockey. I was both Danny Gallivan and Yvan Cournoyer, describing the play-by-play of an electrifying rush leading to a goal with seconds left to play. At the time, there was no organized hockey for girls—only ringette. Later in high school I found a recreational league and laced up every week. In one game, I had a breakaway from the blue line. I was Guy Lafleur, ready to swoop in on the hapless goalie. As I lunged toward the puck, I tripped over the pick of my figure skates, falling flat on my face. Goodbye, figure skates.

Once I bought my prized hockey skates, I had to learn to skate all over again. (I kept falling over the front edges of my pick-less hockey skates.) At McGill, I didn't have the talent to make the varsity women's team. So I played intramural hockey, joining a women's engineering team called the Tachyons (named after a subatomic particle by the lone physicist on the team). Some didn't know how to skate. But that never mattered. We just enjoyed the thrill of hockey. I still remember one pre-game warm-up when I was knocked out cold after colliding head-on with a player from the other team. We had both been skating at full speed in opposite directions, passing a puck the length of the rink to our respective teammates—heads down. You get the picture. Good thing we were playing the med-school team that night.

After moving to Boston for graduate school, I inquired about intramural hockey. There was a league for men, but not for women.

Why not start one? And so, a teetotalling Muslim Canuck introduced women's intramural hockey at Harvard. I was one of the few who could lift the puck off the ice. My friends from California and Florida seemed to have the most fun, even though few knew how to skate. It was the sheer thrill of playing hockey that brought out the smiles.

Now middle-aged, three pregnancies later, I look back wistfully at my hockey-playing days. I am not yet a hockey parent. If I do go down that road, I will look to the example of Daniele Sauvageau—the legendary coach of the Canadian women's Olympic hockey team that won gold in 2002—for maintaining grace and poise under pressure.

I have found other Muslim women who share a passion for hockey, including one friend who recently played for a varsity team in Alberta. On the ice, there was no problem. Hockey equipment lends itself to maintaining modesty in attire, as opposed to say, swimming. It was off the ice where negotiations were made in good faith. Teammates understood when she excused herself from beer outings and the "girls' night out." They went out of their way to help her find a place to pray on road trips. But perhaps the most awkward issue she faced—and one that many observant Muslim women still face—was the casual nudity of the locker room. Modesty is prescribed in Islam, not merely between men and women, but between members of the same gender as well. Locker rooms, showers, open-concept washrooms—all pose challenges to Muslims. Those of us who play sports often dash in and out of dressing rooms, usually with our eyes glued to the floor.

Having completed a season of pond hockey, my kids and I are now ready to play a few weeks of street hockey. The only difference from my childhood days is that now I imagine myself as Hayley Wickenheiser, scoring with only seconds left to play.

There Really Is a Canadian Way

In the Jan/Feb 2007 issue of the US journal *Foreign Affairs*, Dominique Moïsi of the French Institute of International Relations proposed that current world tensions were not symptomatic of a clash of civilizations but rather a result of interdependent layers of conflict.

One such conflict, he argued, is not so much a clash

between Islam and the West but rather increasing tensions between secularism and faith. Polls conducted by the Pew Global Attitudes Project show that the role and importance of religion is declining in the West (with the exception of the United States), while the opposite is true in much of the rest of the world (with the exception of China). In particular, the role of faith in daily life is quite central to many Muslims, whether they live in Europe or in the Muslim world.

Cultural tensions have been evident recently in Canada, as exemplified in rumblings in Quebec about accommodations to the province's Orthodox Jews and Muslims. A national debate has taken place over the niqab, the veil worn by a minuscule proportion of Muslim women. In 2005, Ontario Premier Dalton McGuinty capitulated to an international campaign aimed at banning the use of Islamic principles in family arbitration. These tensions are not going away any time soon.

Another layer of conflict, according to Mr Moïsi, is an emotional clash of cultures. But not culture in the traditional sense. On the one hand, Europe and the United States embody a culture of fear—that is, the discourse focuses on fear of immigration, terrorism, and economic decline. On the other hand, there is a culture of humiliation, predominant in Muslim countries, where many feel they are at the receiving end of an unjust global system. Autocratic governments (often supported by the West) and colonial occupation have formed the daily reality of millions of Muslims over the past few decades. Many also feel that the "war on terror" is, in reality, a war on Islam.

Within these overarching themes, enter Canada, with a contribution so unique, so Canadian, that it has people talking across many divides.

The CBC's *Little Mosque on the Prairie* created an unprecedented worldwide buzz. The brainchild of Zarqa Nawaz, it is a modest attempt to build bridges of understanding by showing Muslims as ordinary Canadians interacting with other ordinary Canadians. Sharp humour is used to whittle away at mutual insecurities. Many Muslims have loved the show, having the confidence to laugh at themselves. A prime-time comedy about their identity signals their integration into the mainstream.

Little Mosque takes aim at many realistic situations. Take for example, the fact that North American Muslims have failed to unite in the determination of the start of Ramadan. The first episode captured this absurdity with poignant hilarity. And while it may seem incredible for someone to mix up "Protestant" with "prostitute," I attended a Friday sermon where a community leader spoke about the arrests of Canadian Muslims in an alleged terrorist plot, saying, "We condone such behaviour, we condone it!" He paused to hear advice from the front row, and resumed his speech: "Sorry— I meant we *condemn* such behaviour." We silently prayed that the informers present in the mosque had a sense of humour.

While disagreements are solved amicably in the quaint rural town of Mercy, perhaps "Sects in the City" best describes the nasty community politics that are always present in any city. And given the number of legal battles between mosque attendees, hiring an ex-lawyer as an imam is not so far-fetched. Real life can be stranger than fiction.

Why are so many rooting for *Little Mosque* to succeed? It embodies that most Canadian of traits: dialogue. We fervently believe that a culture of dialogue transcends the antagonistic cultures of fear and humiliation. It reminds us of the story of Maher Arar, who has experienced the humiliating consequences that can result when a society allows itself to be governed by fear. His success is inspiring, since it shows us that our collective commitment to justice can prevail over fear and humiliation. Mr Arar has graciously paid tribute to the Canadian people for their support, for without it his efforts would have been for naught.

What is it about our Canadian mosaic that fosters the success of people such as Ms Nawaz and Mr Arar in a post-9/11 era? Both are observant Muslims with bold initiatives to change the Canadian landscape for the better. Their plucky efforts have resonated with Canadians nationwide, reflecting a culture of compassionate meritocracy. Yet, we need to be on guard against the erosion of our defining values. A recent study by the Institute for Research on Public Policy shows that visible minority immigrants and their children are less integrated than their white counterparts, due in part to a sense of exclusion. There is enough alienation in the world— let's guard against its growth here.

According to Mr Moïsi, globalization is an accelerant in a tinderbox of potential conflicts. We can instantly know what the "other" says or thinks about us, and react instantly as well. But many of us lack cultural and historical understanding to properly understand reactions in context. Canadians can play a pivotal role in this explosive situation. Our commitment to dialogue, justice, and compassion can go a long way, both at home and abroad.

Looking to the Charter

"Whereas Canada is founded upon principles that recognize the supremacy of God and the rule of law." So begins the Charter of Rights and Freedoms, signed on April 17, 1982. Perhaps a surprise to some, given our self-image as a secular nation.

Drafted in the shadow of the War Measures Act, the

Charter seeks to limit the powers of the government from encroaching on the rights of individuals. It has served as a model for the bills of rights adopted by South Africa and New Zealand.

In the post-9/11 era of global tensions, why not envision the export of Charter principles to the Muslim world? The Canadian government has made human rights and good governance the centrepiece of its response to the 2004 House of Commons Foreign Affairs Committee report, *Exploring Canada's Relations with the Countries of the Muslim World*. The response asserts that "Islam upholds pluralism, including the liberal-democratic precepts of equal rights for women and minorities." The reality differs from country to country.

Historically, Muslims point to the Constitution of Medina, written in 622 CE, which established a pluralistic state based on the principles of equality, consensual governance, and pluralism. These ideals served as the foundation of Islamic rule in Spain for seven centuries. More recently, Indonesia—the world's largest Muslim nation—has transformed peacefully from dictatorship to multiparty democracy. Problems still exist, but the prognosis is hopeful. Canada has helped in this transition by providing human-rights expertise.

Exporting Charter principles to the Muslim world is not only laudable but also achievable, as the essence of human dignity is germane to Islam. The language of human rights is a natural starting point for a common understanding between Canada and Muslims worldwide.

Given the importance of human rights in the Islamic ethos both in the past and the present, one would think that Muslims have much to contribute to the new Museum of Human Rights. Furthermore, a community in the eye of a human-rights storm would be empowered by becoming a bona fide partner in a project whose mission is to trace the evolution of human rights, with a focus on the Canadian experience. Yet not one single Muslim sits on the museum's advisory council. Suitable candidates include Liberal Senator Mobina Jaffer, human-rights activist Monia Mazigh, and journalist Haroon Siddiqui. Instead, the council's chair promises to be "more active" with groups without representation, saying that a "100 person" board would be unwieldy. Imagine, a human rights museum that finds human diversity unwieldy, opting instead for a two-tiered system of representation.

Nevertheless, the Charter should be honoured. In times of tribulation, Canadian Muslims will look to it for the protection of their rights. They could invoke it for internal disputes. For example, a challenge should be mounted against any Muslim organization that denies women the right to vote in general elections.

The best way to honour the Charter is to apply it for the advancement of justice.

Facing New Identities

At one level, it seems like an absurd sketch featuring Mary Walsh and Cathy Jones from *This Hour Has 22 Minutes*: normally placid Canadians forced to confront their fuzzy notions of identity by two outspoken Muslim women.

Stereotypes are turned on their heads as Canadians wax passionately about citizenship and passports, while each woman, speaking in her own name, discards the cloak of submissiveness too often associated with her religion. If only reality were as simple as fiction.

The Muslim women are Maha Elsamnah and Monia Mazigh—two very different individuals whose public ordeals have forced Canadians to reflect on fundamental values of this nation. They also represent two faces (among many) of Muslim participation in Western democracies, giving rise to a long overdue reflection on an ethic of citizenship.

Ms Elsamnah has raised the ire of many Canadians. Some have called for the revocation of her citizenship. The anger is fuelled by her support of Osama bin Laden and the al-Qaeda mass murder of September 11, 2001, her contempt for Canada's social environment as a place to raise her children, and her gall in using the very system she professes to hate.

It has been pointed out that however objectionable her views, our laws do not strip individuals of citizenship for holding repugnant opinions. While it may seem galling to abuse the many privileges of citizenship (passports, access to health care, etc.), Ms Elsamnah is certainly not alone in claiming these privileges as a matter of convenience. The list includes business investors and Florida snowbirds.

In contrast, Monia Mazigh won widespread admiration for her tireless, dignified campaign to have her husband Maher Arar returned from Syria. She has made good use of democratic institutions to achieve justice, so that her children will not grow up bitter about their father's ordeal. Against insurmountable odds, she has fought for basic democratic principles such as the rule of law and government accountability.

Following on her belief that Canada is a land of justice and opportunity, Ms Mazigh ran for elections in 2004 to contribute to the evolution of these ideals. It is a shame that Ms Mazigh's story has not been widely publicized in the Muslim world, for it reflects how our democratic institutions, with all their imperfections, can serve as instruments of change. The fact that a Muslim woman can engage in and win a public campaign to have her husband's wrongful deportation overturned; that her effort wins national respect; that alleged police wrongdoing in the deportation become the subject of a government inquiry; and that she becomes a bona fide candidate in a national election—all these speak volumes about the fundamental nature of Canada as a place where an individual, regardless of gender, creed, or ethnic origin can strive for justice, a claim few nations can make.

The divergent paths of Maha and Monia should give pause to Muslims living in Western democracies about their own participation in society. Does an oath of citizenship take precedence over allegiance to Muslim causes elsewhere, right or wrong?

(This issue isn't confined to Muslims; a good friend related her discomfort with a family rabbi who asked her son at his bar mitzvah whether his primary allegiance lay with Israel or Canada.)

Islamic jurisprudence regards citizenship as a sacred contract between a Muslim and the state. Muslims who choose to make their homes in non-Islamic countries must honour the duties of this contract. The rights and duties of citizenship are not to be taken lightly; rights should be demanded truthfully, duties discharged faithfully. As well, it is a Muslim's duty to strive for the preservation of belief, life, and security in one's immediate environment. This is combined with the Koranic directive that believers should be witnesses for God, standing up for justice, whether on behalf of oneself or others. Justice must be the overriding constant in every situation and in every encounter.

It is incumbent upon Muslims to implement these basic Koranic tenets. Canadian Muslims should abide not by the creed "my tribe, right or wrong," but by allegiance to the principles of universal justice demanded by their faith. There are Muslims who are unjust, and Prophet Muhammad counselled to "help your brother whether he is oppressed or an oppressor," explaining that one must help the latter by stopping his oppression.

Turning a blind eye to community members who exhort extreme views is antithetical to the Koranic exhortation to promote what is good and forbid the wrong, for extreme views create fear and insecurity. Canadian Muslims should continue to denounce those who advocate distrust, hate, and violence; and they should take part in bettering society. To care primarily for one's own well-being, to be uninterested in wider public issues, is in stark contrast to the Koran's universal message and the Prophet Muhammad's example—to strive towards improving conditions for all of humanity.

Given the great emphasis Islam places on education, charity and justice, there are ample opportunities to work towards a better Canada in order to fulfill one's deep convictions, for example, about child poverty, aboriginal rights, and the future of health care. It is high time for an internal debate. For a community whose faith emphasizes a universal rather than parochial world-view, will it be a "ghetto" or "get-go" mentality?

Make Room for the Spiritual in Educating Our Young

In Grade 1, I used to sing "God Save the Queen" every morning at my Montreal public school. I would also stand in silence while the class recited the Lord's Prayer. We rounded off our morning routine with an off-key yet heartfelt rendition of "O Canada."

Later on, I transferred to another public school where we sang "O Canada" only. I quickly forgot about praying for the Queen. Yet I sorely missed beginning my day reflecting upon the majesty of God. In Grade 1, I didn't pray to Jesus (he is regarded as a prophet in Islam) but to God alone. It had been a perfect way to start the day, in peace and humility.

Now the only way to recite communal prayers in Ontario schools is to enroll in faith-based education, which currently receives no government funding—unless you're Catholic. Ontario's Catholic population was granted this right in the British North America Act of 1867. However, multiculturalism and the Charter of Rights arrived in the twentieth century. Non-Christian groups have been demanding a tiny sliver of the same government funding pie. Even the United Nations has ruled Ontario's Catholic-only educational funding policy to be discriminatory.

The issue remained dormant until 2007, when Ontario Conservative leader John Tory made a pre-election promise to level the playing field for those opting for non-Catholic religious schools. The Liberals quickly warned about diverting precious funds from a public system under repair. Then came Premier Dalton McGuinty's dire prediction of the unravelling of social cohesion if the government funded religious schools. According to this logic, Alberta, Manitoba and Quebec are doomed to produce ghettoes of insular communities on the cusp of social upheavals. Not to be outdone, the "God delusion" crowd has added a dollop of French laïcité to its morning latté, insisting on the atheism of public money. Not a penny should be given to religious schools, they argue. Let them subsist on sub-prime loans.

On the face of it, the issue is one of fairness. Why is only one religious group entitled to public money, while others are shut out? Other provinces have found ways to fund religious schools, making them more accountable and standardized by bringing them within the purview of the public system. Public schools have not crumbled, nor has there been a mass exodus to religious schools. But parents have more viable choices in how they educate their children.

Like those of other faiths, some Canadian Muslims wish to

place their children in educational environments where they will imbibe religious values in harmony with their Canadian identity. There are Muslim schools in every major Canadian city, and the numbers are growing. These schools provide an environment conducive to daily prayer. During Ramadan, the schedule is eased for students who are fasting. A modicum of modesty (in dress and behaviour) is expected on the part of all students. Of course, it is not always easy to run such schools. Some have financial problems, others can't find qualified teachers. Student discipline is sometimes a problem.

Despite these obstacles, Muslim and other religious schools seek to nurture children's spiritual and moral lives. Does the public system have the luxury or the mandate to allow such exploration of spirituality? Most would answer no. Yet Quebec, the most secular province in the country, is about to embark on an innovative program that will allow students to do just that.

Looking back to my own schooling, I was not emotionally scarred by the morning prayers in Grade 1. Neither was my best friend, a Hindu, who chose to opt out. Listening to the Lord's Prayer allowed me to relate to the spiritual calling of a faith different from my own—an experience that has served me well throughout life. And singing "God Save the Queen" instilled a sense of respect for authority.

I am a byproduct of an excellent public school system that taught me that there is strength in diversity and to respect differences. If there was one shortcoming, it was the lack of time allotted for spiritual reflection. As a parent, I would like to provide my children with every opportunity for this.

The issue of funding for religious schools deserves to be studied in a calm, detailed manner. We must avoid politically motivated rhetoric and stop stigmatizing those who want this option. If adults cannot work together to find a reasonable compromise, what kind of example are we setting for our children?

China's Hui and a
Muslim Model for Canada

Seek knowledge, even if in
China, for the seeking of
knowledge is incumbent upon every Muslim.

While Muslim scholars dispute the origin of this narration (or hadith), often attributed to the Prophet Muhammad, they are unanimous about its message: Muslims (male and female) are obliged to seek knowledge, even if it entails extensive travel. Incredibly, this narration may point toward a successful integration model for Muslim communities in the West.

Recent tensions prompt these questions: can secular democracies successfully integrate Muslims keen on asserting their religious identity? Can Muslim minorities successfully adapt to their host societies without compromising cherished values? The answers, according to Umar Faruq Abd-Allah of the Nawawi Foundation in Chicago, may be found in China.

In his view, the integration of China's Hui Muslim minority offers a valuable template for Muslim diasporas in the West. For centuries, the Hui enjoyed independence and economic strength, rooted in a confident, indigenous Islamic culture. They have played an important role in their country's history, while maintaining social solidarity and a deep sense of being simultaneously Muslim and Chinese.

The Hui are culturally distinct from their Uighur coreligionists of western China; their ingenuity lay in their ability to think outside the Semitic Abrahamic box. Armed with deep knowledge of Islamic traditions and ancient Chinese civilization, they found common ground with Confucianism, Taois, and Buddhism. They developed language, cultural paradigms, and institutions that bridged the two worlds, to create a vibrant culture that was wholly Chinese and Muslim. Hui scholars did not deconstruct the Chinese ethos; rather, they built on the best of Chinese traditions.

The sixteenth century saw the emergence of a unique institution: the nusi—mosques for women, run by women. These continue to thrive today, as do the ahong—Muslim female clerics (or imams) who provide spiritual and educational guidance to men and women. The ahong are trained in both Islamic knowledge and Chinese culture.

The evolution of the Hui reflects the cultural diversity of Muslims worldwide. Wherever they went, Muslims formulated distinctive indigenous forms of culture rooted in the teachings of their faith. It is incorrect to assume that the only authentic form of Muslim cultural expression is Middle Eastern.

The example of the Hui should impel Canadian Muslims to reflect on the evolution of their institutions—many of which reflect the mentality of "hislam" and autocracy prevalent in the Arab world and South Asia. There are already signs of an impending collision between gender equity and the authoritarian patriarchy entrenched in many of the country's Muslim institutions. Many Muslim women have embraced the self-empowerment offered by Canadian society, fighting back with knowledge and research in Islamic traditions to demand equality. Others are turning away from institutions that are dismissive, if not hostile, to their concerns.

The issue of gender equity is but one cultural value that will play a key role in the establishment of an indigenous Canadian Muslim culture. Freedom of conscience, freedom of expression, critical inquiry, and pluralism must be incorporated by Muslims into their lives if they are to thrive in Canada. So must a respectful appreciation of the best Canadian traditions. The good news is that classical Islamic thought already provides the foundation to incorporate these fundamental values into a paradigm that is Muslim and Canadian. The question is, who recognizes the urgency to do so?

A Leader Who Knows How to Serve

"A leader is a servant of the people," said Prophet Muhammad fourteen centuries ago. This maxim formed the foundation of governance during the first few decades of the Islamic empire, but thereafter, it was applied unevenly as Islam spread from the shores of Spain to China. Moral governance usually led to lengthy tenure, despotic rule crumbled.

Some would argue that today the spirit and letter of the Prophet's words have been pretty much abandoned in many Muslim countries. Some would even add that current leaders are servants not so much of their own people as of the United States. Yet the above maxim is universal and has relevance in Canada. It sets a condition for leadership—the service of people. It defines leadership not in terms of self-interest but in terms of the greater good. As an electorate, we hope our leaders take this idea to heart. We hope that such a noble ideal forms the core of the social contract between elected leaders and the electorate.

The converse is also true: those who truly serve people are seen as leaders by those whom they serve.

There is a third interpretation of this simple, yet profound phrase—namely, that people are actually masters over their leaders. While Canadians generally eschew hierarchical class distinctions, this interpretation should be seen in light of the empowerment it offers an electorate. We are not helpless sheep at the mercy of powerful political wolves.

This message hit home when, as part of a political panel, I was asked to name the high and low points of the 2005 spring parliamentary session. There were many lows in that fractious House, but I thought the lowest occurred when our leaders refrained from sending representatives to the Netherlands on V-E Day. No-confidence motions hung like a noose, making the parliamentary body count an issue of political survival. Everybody had to be in Ottawa—even if that meant no one could be in Europe.

The sacrifice and honour of Canadian soldiers were deemed secondary to political machinations. After the public expressed its disgust, the party leaders finally did the right thing and travelled overseas to pay proper tribute to the legacy of a self-sacrificing generation. Our leaders served the demands of the people.

The high point, in my mind, was the noble example of the late Chuck Cadman. Here was a man, dying of cancer, who nonetheless served the interests of his Surrey North constituents. The trip to Ottawa from British Columbia is exhausting for those in the best of health. Imagine Mr Cadman's commitment: During the nail-biting parliamentary vote on the budget in May 2004, almost everyone voted along party lines. Mr Cadman, an independent, was wooed by all sides, but he consulted his constituents to see how he should vote. The former Reform/Canadian Alliance stalwart voted with the Liberals—respecting the wishes of constituents, who did not want an election. With the fate of so many on his shoulders, he remained a true servant of his people, a true leader.

In both instances, the electorate dictated the course of

action of our leaders.

Whether it is health care, child poverty, or US-Canada relations, or some other issue, it is up to us to push the envelope on what matters to us. We are one of the few fortunate nations on Earth with the capacity to make government work for the benefit of the people. As the saying goes, use it or lose it.

Democracy, Peace, and Sharia Law

In December, 2006, the polling firm Environics surveyed 500 adult Muslims across Canada on questions relating to their experiences living in Canada. The results were accurate to within plus or minus 4.4 percentage points (in 19 out of 20 samples). The demographic statistics revealed a diverse Muslim population, belying the notion of a singular Muslim community.

The survey found that 45 percent of Canadian Muslims possess a university degree (or higher), compared with 33 percent of the general population. At the time, 94 percent of those surveyed were proud of being Canadian, citing the policies of democracy, multiculturalism, peace, and humanitarianism. When asked what they liked least, the majority replied: "weather and taxes." Only 6 percent cited Canada's foreign policy.

While security issues present challenges to social cohesion, the Environics survey revealed trends among the "weather and taxes" Muslims that may test our multicultural model in the years to come. This majority believe that they are treated better here than in any other Western country; that the quality of life for Muslim women is better here than anywhere else (including most Muslim countries); that Canadians are less hostile to Islam when compared to Europeans; and that they are willing to adopt Canadian customs.

Forty-four percent of Canadian Muslims believe Canada should accommodate their traditional beliefs, while 81 percent of the general population thinks immigrants should adopt mainstream Canadian beliefs. In particular, 53 percent of Muslims think sharia law should be recognized as a legal basis for settling family disputes, while an overwhelming majority of the general population disagrees. Of those surveyed, 55 percent of Muslim women and 59 percent of Muslims aged 18 to 29 indicate their preference for sharia law. Remember, this survey was conducted one year after the Ontario sharia controversy.

These numbers suggest that the use of sharia in Canada is by no means a dead issue, even if sharia arbitration courts have been deemed illegal in many provinces. Just look at Britain, where the government has been grappling with the role of sharia in family law. The popularity of informal "Islamic courts"—which have no standing in British law— has been growing steadily there. Most cases involve women seeking divorce. Since these "courts" are outside the legal system, there is no accountability, review, or transparency in the judgments, and no formal standards or training for the judges, who are exclusively male. Some have received training in Saudi Arabia, where a conservative form of Islam is prevalent. In domestic violence cases, Islamic scholars have hesitated to dissolve abusive marriages, leaving wives too intimidated to pursue charges. In one case, a judge declined to grant divorce to a victim of domestic violence. Her father then came forward in support of her, at which point the judge reversed his decision, highlighting the central role of the family patriarch in such proceedings.

The British situation illustrates that if sharia is driven underground in Canada, quasi-courts will proliferate in response to demand, without the necessary checks and balances. Given the growing affinity to sharia here, there will be future debate on this topic. Instead of the hysteria of 2005 in Ontario, we will need then to engage in rational discourse about the flexibility of sharia, identities in flux, the role of religious belief in family law, and the balance between religious freedom and gender equality. In spite of reassurances by proponents, traditional Islamic law contradicts gender equality in inheritance and divorce.

Why the growing affinity to sharia? Since 9/11, Canadian Muslims have felt increased discrimination. This has a direct impact on identity and how a minority perceives its acceptance by the majority. With the raucous, sometimes racist, nature of the Ontario controversy, many Muslims were forced to focus on sharia as a component of identity, resulting in a plurality wishing to abide by Islamic principles in matters of family law.

Making Islamic arbitration illegal will not make it vanish. Without proper oversight of informal sharia courts, we risk ending up with a mess like Britain's.

There's Nothing Like Watching the Montreal Canadiens Up Close

Recently, I took my son to a Habs game at the Bell Centre in Montreal. I had offered my two daughters equal opportunity; they declined, preferring to wait for Stars on Ice.

The Carolina Hurricanes were in town. My son was excited to see one of the talented Stahl brothers in action. Don't ask me which one. We decided to go early, to catch the pregame skate. I chose a route that passed the old Montreal Forum, so I could explain to him how special the building was. Here we had witnessed the passionate "battles for Quebec" between the Quebec Nordiques and the Canadiens. There were the nights when the crowd roared "Guy! Guy!" as Lafleur rushed down the ice, leaving hapless defenders in his wake. I told him about the hush that would fall in awe of Jean Béliveau's poise under pressure. French. English. It didn't matter, it was the home of champions.

I reminisced how the Canadiens won the Stanley Cup year after year in the 1970s. We'd line up along Ste-Catherine Street to see the annual parade. How proud we felt as a city, host to a team that celebrated excellence. I felt a shiver. And then I smiled, remembering an anecdote about the final game in the hallowed Forum.

Some friends had bought nosebleed seats from a scalper. Rising for the national anthem, they heard the unforgettable voice of the late Roger Doucet. Unfamiliar with the team's history, they didn't realize they were listening to a recording. They looked everywhere for the man. The next day, my friend complained that Mr Doucet was nowhere to be seen. I explained why, much to my friend's chagrin.

My son and I drove into a parking lot near the Bell Centre. The attendant assumed I was there for shopping, and asked if I was leaving soon. "I plan to stay until the end of the game," I answered much to his surprise. He probably hadn't seen a woman in hijab attend an NHL game. As I went to pay, another attendant asked me where I was from. "India," I replied, "but I grew up in Montreal and love hockey." He smiled, "Well, my sister, as-salamu alaykum. Enjoy the game." I think he was from Lebanon. Imagine, a Muslim from India and one from the Middle East exchanging pleasantries over hockey. Only in Canada, eh?

My son and I walked through the snow, coughing as we passed the smokers outside. The atmosphere inside was electric. And smoke-free. Vendors were selling the Canadiens program, reminding me of my childhood trips to the Forum. The glossy pages of our hockey heroes, replete with statistics, had seemed larger than life.

As we wound through the crowd, we passed by the portraits of past Hab greats. The Richards. Béliveau. Mahovlich. Cournoyer. My son was drawn to the Rocket. I had told him about my collection of hockey cards. "Do you have the Rocket?" he asked eagerly. "I'm not that old," I replied with some dismay. Nothing deflates the female ego more than having to say those words.

We made our way to our seats, not far from goalie phenom Carey Price. We watched the pregame skate intently, soaking in the whoosh of skates, the crisp slapshots, the ripple of the net. The players glided effortlessly on the ice, preparing for a showdown. What magic! After they left, the Zambonis prepared the ice to near perfection. To kill time, we compared the Bell Centre to Scotiabank Place, home of the Ottawa Senators. Just two weeks before, my son had seen a nail-biter between the Sens and his favourite team, the Pittsburgh Penguins, featuring his favourite player, Sidney Crosby. We decided that the Bell Centre was larger and more entertaining. It also had all those Stanley Cup banners.

We stood for the national anthems. I sang "The Star Spangled Banner" solemnly, remembering my trips to Boston's Fenway Park as a grad student. During "O Canada," I teared up. It always happens. At my kids' schools. On Canada Day. At hockey games. I don't know why; those chords resonate deeply in my soul.

Finally, the puck was dropped. The crowd roared. End-to-end action. Deft puck handling. Speed. No game is more stirring. Unfortunately, the Habs were no match for the 'Canes that evening. They lost 5-1. During the third period, the boo-birds came out in full force. Hell hath no fury like disappointed Montreal hockey fans.

After we returned to my mother's home, I found my suitcase of hockey and baseball cards from the 1970s. I pulled out one that combined my son's love for hockey and for Timbits: a Pittsburgh Penguin by the name of Tim Horton. Now if I could only find Sidney Crosby's card to save for my future grandchildren.

The Rights of Women

Putting Women First

The competing demands of religious traditions and the rights of modern women appear to put multiculturalism and feminism on opposite sides.

While Islamic and Jewish traditions are at the centre of these conflicts, similar battles have occurred involving Christains in the near past, and continue to occur. With a resurgence of religious expression in many Western countries, we are bound to witness more such collisions. The banning of visible religious symbols in France, for example, is the combined result of an orthodox secular foundation, a failure to implement inclusive immigration policies, and a reflection of historical tensions between Europe and Islam.

Canada has a relatively young multiculturalism policy and an even younger Charter. Thus far, both have served to build a relatively inclusive society. We have not yet seen the appearance of dangerous fissures that have emerged in some European countries. Canadians are inclusive—up to a point. A poll published by the Trudeau Foundation in 2002 shows that the majority of Canadians value immigrants (75 percent believe that Muslims make a valuable contribution to society) and reject the notion of race-based immigration or screening at the ports of entry.

Nonetheless, when it comes to multiculturalism versus equality rights, 81 percent believe the latter should prevail.

One of the most thoughtful essays on this topic was written by University of Toronto professor Janice Stein. In the September 2006 issue of *The Literary Review of Canada*, she asked the question: When multiculturalism and equality rights clash, whose values prevail?

Professor Stein relates her own struggle to be recognized as an equal within her synagogue. Frustrated at the glacial pace of change, she refuses to be satisfied with the rabbinical advice to be patient, or the language of "separate, but inclusive." While she acknowledges the freedom to choose a more liberal congregation, she raises a fundamental question: How is it possible for religious institutions to receive tax exemptions while they practise discrimination against women?

What makes Professor Stein's approach so refreshing is her honesty in addressing the tensions within her own tradition first, and using that as a basis to consider broader implications. Contrast that with those commentators who rush to uphold the civilized nature of the West by condemning the barbarity of the rest. If an imam in Australia equates immodestly dressed women with meat, they heap scorn on Muslim culture in its entirety. If the South Asian community in British Columbia has the courage to address spousal abuse in public, the finger-pointers waste no time in making generalizations about South Asian culture. Their hubris is only matched by a collective amnesia of struggles right here. Not long ago, Canadian judges made connections between immodest clothing and rape. Spousal abuse remained a taboo topic until a few decades ago.

Ignorant remarks about a woman's state of dress are abhorrent, whether uttered by an imam or a Canadian judge. They reflect an abuse of power, not the moral dereliction of an entire group.

While the Trudeau Foundation poll is a heartening reminder of the fairness of Canadians, it also provides an opportunity for Muslims to reflect upon gender issues within their community. Of the 37 percent of Canadians who have a negative view of Islam, 21 percent cite the treatment of Muslim women as the basis for their views. While some

Muslims may blame the media coverage of these issues, the reality is that gender relations often fall far short of Koranic imperatives. Just recently, a director of the Islamic Society of North America (Canada), told the *Toronto Star*: "I think if a woman is so pretty that she would attract attention to her, then she should cover her face," adding, "It's essentially trying to avoid any bad feelings from men."

Such a view is contrary to that of Prophet Muhammad. Shortly before his death, the Prophet travelled with a trusted companion named Al Fadl. During their trip, they passed a group of women. Al Fadl began to stare at the face of one who is described as "beautiful." The Prophet physically turned Al Fadl's face away. He stared again. The Prophet repeated his gesture. He did not order the woman to cover her face. He placed the onus on the man to refrain from gazing, in compliance with Koranic directives. How, then, can a Muslim leader (in Australia or Canada) usurp the Prophetic model that placed emphasis on personal responsibility? Muslim women and men have a duty to challenge such views head-on.

The poll results lead us to wonder: Is our Canadian tent big enough to accommodate a diversity of views? And whose definition of equality should prevail? There are no easy answers—only further opportunities to engage in rich debate about our defining values.

Storming the Harvard Bastion

The comments by Harvard president Lawrence Summers in 2005 about "innate" gender differences in the mathematical sciences may have caused outrage, but they weren't all that surprising. Like golf, Harvard and the "hard" sciences have been the bastion of men for quite some time. It is only in the past few decades that women have significantly entered a zone previously forbidden.

I entered Harvard graduate school in 1983 to pursue a PhD in chemical physics. Only a handful of female students formed the incoming class of about twenty-five. The only female faculty member in chemistry was an assistant professor. Rumour had it that one big-name prof in organic chemistry refused to take any female graduate students. In my six years there, his research group remained an exclusive men's club. He later went on to win a Nobel Prize.

One of my classmates was a whiz, entering Harvard at twenty and leaving with a PhD at twenty-four. She was also an exceptional seamstress and baseball player. I wonder where she would fit into Dr Summers's view of the world.

We never felt inferior—or superior—to our male counterparts. We just loved science. Somewhere along the line, we had been inspired to pursue our dream, to use our God-given inquisitiveness to explore the wonders of creation, and be given the opportunity to do so. The naysayers only served to strengthen our resolve to seek knowledge.

In my case, the criticism also came from a few men of the Harvard Islamic Society. "A good Muslim woman," one male PhD candidate told me, "shouldn't study for a PhD." He also occasionally gave the Friday sermon. As the only woman in attendance for a number of years, I would hear, on one hand, how Islam honoured women, and on the other, how we were created inferior to men.

At one point I thought that if my religion relegated me to second-class status as a human being by virtue of the way I was created, then I wanted no part of it. Inherently, I knew that God was just. After much soul-searching and reading, I came to realize that the chauvinistic views held by many Muslims were in direct conflict with the teachings of Islam and the example of the first generation of Muslims, considered as the best. I came to learn that a Muslim woman was the founder of Islamic jurisprudence and that, in the early days of Islam, women went into battle, questioned the Prophet Muhammad, wrote poetry, pronounced judgments and were bona fide scholars. Which invites the question: What happened?

That question deserves to be studied without the usual reflexive blame put on colonialism. Or the usual defensive posture of shielding scholars' writings from criticism. The writings of many venerated scholars from the Indian subcontinent contain insulting views about women: we are deemed lacking in intelligence, maturity, and ability; our mere presence is a temptation to men.

One line of thinking proceeds from outright rejection of the secular basis of Western thought and the wholesale acceptance of obscure Western clinical research. Using this research in combination with obscure prophetic narrations, these scholars provide religious legitimacy for views that "prove" women are stupid by nature; untrustworthy basket cases incapable of holding a job during menstruation; and, for some, in need of a good beating from time to time.

It will not be surprising to hear Lawrence Summers's words repeated by those who are critical of the West. "Even the president of Harvard says that women are not as good at math as men," some Muslims will declare, in order to prove the inferiority of women, maintaining their subjugation with regards to education. They are oblivious to their own history, in which, for example, Aisha (the Prophet Muhammad's youngest wife) would be consulted for her ability to perform complicated inheritance calculations.

In the end, whether it is a religious authority or the president of Harvard making wholesale generalizations about the inherent nature of women, it is important for women themselves not to feel obliged to fit the stereotype. In secular terms, call this attitude "believing in oneself." In religious terms, it is knowing that my destiny is in the hands of a merciful, compassionate, all-powerful Creator who is the bestower of talents. Myopic pronouncements by men about my innate abilities are ignorant at best. Yet, uttered by men in power they are harmful—for they legitimize the denial of the rightful opportunity of women to learn and contribute to society.

Cynthia Friend, the lone female faculty member in the early eighties, was Harvard's chair of chemistry and chemical biology from 2004 to 2007. Back in 1983, she would often bring her two small children to the department, as if to say: "My role as a mother is not something to hide at work." Her example made quite an impression. So have the efforts of Muslim women in early history. Inspired by examples of the past, the future never looked brighter.

Sharia-phobia

Sharia is an Arabic word that means "a path to water," the source of life. For Muslims, it is a comprehensive framework of justice based on the Koran and the examples from the life of Prophet Muhammad. Sharia's aim is five-fold: protection of life, faith, wealth, intellect, and progeny. Sharia has been around for fourteen centuries, exists in numerous cultures, and given rise to at least five recognized schools of jurisprudence. It covers such disparate fields as economics, criminal justice, international relations, and family matters. The study of sharia is so important that in the 1990s Harvard law school launched an Islamic legal studies program.

Yet many Canadians have opted for a more facile description: sharia, bad. *Globe* columnist Lysiane Gagnon puts it in the same category as incest. Anti-sharia activist Homa Arjomand has called for the imprisonment of sharia advocates. And Quebec MNA Fatima Houda-Pepin—ripping a page from what might be called "The Protocols of the Elders of Mecca"—continues to warn about the international conspiracy of Islamists using compliant Quebec media outlets. It's the same mantra she used a decade ago, dismissing those of us who campaigned for the right to wear the hijab as unwitting pawns of those same Islamists. Great fodder for Jon Stewart and *The Daily Show*—except that no one is laughing.

Undoubtedly, sharia-phobia skewed the debate over Ontario faith-based arbitration to such a frenzied level that lies were perpetuated as facts, paranoia as patriotism. Just as the neoconservative lobby in the United States peddled the bogus threat of Iraqi WMD, our own neosecularists (including several Muslims) brazenly peddled Muslim family law as an existential threat to Western liberal democracy. As in the case of Iraq, the audience was a fearful and already biased public ready to accept the sensational media accounts.

And it worked. Like the French decision to ban "conspicuous" religious symbols in public schools, Ontario Premier Dalton McGuinty's decision to ban all faith-based arbitration was aimed primarily at Muslims. Other religions were included to provide a veneer of fairness. At least the Quebec Legislature had the candour to express its animosity toward sharia alone, remaining silent on all other faiths.

Not so, you protest, there are legitimate issues of debate. Yes, but consider the following: in the operation of Jewish, Aboriginal, and Ismaili arbitration tribunals, the issues of "one law for all Ontarians," of "parallel justice systems," and the "ghettoization of minority groups" were never raised by the public. Why all the hue and cry when Muslims wish to avail themselves of the same rights as their fellow Ontarians?

And for those who view this as a victory for the protection of women—think again. There are too many unqualified, ignorant imams making back-alley pronouncements on the lives of women, men, and children. The practice will continue, without any regulation, oversight, or accountability. Muslim women (and men) will still seek religious divorces and settlement of inheritance matters in accordance with their faith. And not just the ubiquitous downtrodden immigrant Muslim woman who speaks little English. Our overburdened courts will still need to rely on experts in Muslim family law to deal with pre-nuptial contracts. Nothing has really changed—except for the fact that we have missed a golden opportunity to shine light on abuses masquerading as faith, and to ensure that rulings don't contradict the Charter of Rights and Freedoms.

Despite the acrimony surrounding the debate, there have been a few silver linings. First is the vigorous discussion that began within the Muslim community about the practicality (or lack thereof) of establishing such tribunals. Unlike rabbis and priests, there is no college of imams in Canada to provide accreditation. There are no institutes to train jurists in Muslim family law. Many Muslim women are ignorant about their own rights within Islam, schooled as they were in cultural misogyny. And certain provisions—such as inheritance shares between sons and daughters—raise concerns of contradicting the Charter. There would have been no shame for community leaders to say: "While we acknowledge our right to arbitration, we admit that we are not ready. We need first to educate our community so its members can make informed choices." But even those who had doubts about Muslim tribunals were stung by the shrill language of the detractors and the abrupt ban by Mr McGuinty.

Beneath the fear-mongering, however, lie fundamental

issues that speak to our identity and values as Canadians. While we treasure the diversity of our population as a strength, a Globe/CTV poll indicated in 2005 that 69 percent of Canadians believed that immigrants should be encouraged to integrate and become part of the broader society rather than maintain their ethnic identity and culture. Interestingly, a poll by the Pew Charitable Trust showed that 60 percent of Canadians believe that Muslims wanted to remain distinct from the broader society. This is not a healthy situation, and requires tough, honest discourse—not the hyperbole we have just witnessed.

The other divide has to do with the place of faith in our society. Neo-secularists have their sights set on religious schools, faith-based lending institutions, and "conspicuous" religious symbols. The majority of Canadians, like their European counterparts, do not ascribe an important role to faith in God. Yet in last year's landmark case before the Supreme Court of Canada of Syndicat Northcrest v. Anselem, the Evangelical Fellowship of Canada and the Seventh-Day Adventist Church in Canada as interveners stated that "the ability to freely express one's faith and one's connection with a religious community are as essential to human dignity as are food or shelter."

Will the banning of all faith-based tribunals violate this principle? Consider that Orthodox Jews must abide by the Beit Din (rabbinical courts). We must continue to find ways to accommodate the sacred and the secular that respect the basic human impulse of faith.

Perhaps the McGuinty decision reflects the prevailing attitude of the majority. However, the way in which it was pronounced was shameful. A principled, detailed statement would have been far more satisfactory than the terse comments issued late Sunday on the fourth anniversary of 9/11.

Yes, criticism would have still ensued. But at least the premier would not have left the impression that Islamophobia has a role in setting public policy.

Banning Hijab: the New Colonialism

The land of *liberté, egalité et fraternité* has taken a decidedly selective definition of these ideals. The banning of all forms of visible religious symbols in state schools (except for discrete pendants) is ostensibly based on France's secular foundations; it can be viewed, however, as a result of a secular orthodoxy, a mirror image of religious extremism that the nation purports to oppose. The target of the ban clearly is the hijab, a visible symbol of France's five-million strong Muslim community, to whom French officialdom essentially present a Bushian choice: you are either with us, or against us. There is even the patronizing arrogance of Bernard Stasi, head of the commission on secularism in French society, who called banning the hijab "a chance for Islam to save itself."

France—having once colonized the people of Algeria, Tunisia, Morocco, Syria, and Lebanon—will now attempt the same on its own shores. The French model of colonization was to strip away the indigenous identities of its subjects, replacing language and culture with that of the motherland. It never succeeded, however, in turning people away from Islam.

The most vocal opponents of the hijab have been so-called feminists who have decided that the Muslim headscarf is a symbol of women's oppression and subjugation. Irrelevant is the voice of Muslim women themselves who choose to abide by the precepts of modesty required by their faith. Feminism, which is about empowering women to make their own choices, now falls prey to the very dictates it once battled. Within certain extreme Muslim circles, a woman's voice is never to be heard in public, and her intellect is deemed deficient. Ironically French feminists seem to agree with these views, as far as Muslim women are concerned, having decided how they must dress, without any respect for their own thoughts on the matter. Call it imperial feminism.

The debate also centres on the role of religion in the public sphere.

France has decided to take the path of strict separation between church and state. Germany is also grappling with the growing presence of the hijab, with battles under way to ban it altogether for government employees. In Italy, a local court upheld a complaint (brought by a Muslim) to forbid the display of a school crucifix, much to the horror of most Italians, including the local Muslim community. All of these policies are on a collision course with Article 9 of the European Convention on Human Rights, which guarantees the right to freedom of religion.

Given the history of religion and state in Europe, it is not surprising that issues of faith cause so much consternation. Throw in a few centuries of colonial rule and former subjects who demand rights to their religious identity as citizens of the motherland. How then do societies balance the rights and interests of various groups? While there is no easy answer, the best policy is one that is attuned to the changing dynamics of the population. As long as there is give and take, there is hope for all to live together with mutual respect. Absolute decrees only serve to alienate.

Indeed, the rejectionists on both sides of the debate are happy with the French ruling. Those trying to improve relations between West and East, trying to convince Muslims that the West is not their enemy, will now have an uphill battle.

The situation in France will have repercussions in Quebec. In 1994, the first Muslim schoolgirl was expelled for wearing the hijab. At the time, the arguments presented by those who would ban the hijab mirrored those in France. The fear of the bloody Algerian civil war spilling onto the shores of Marseilles, suddenly translated into fundamentalism on the shores of the Saint-Lawrence.

Then, as now, the hijab was seen as a symbol of women's oppression, militant Islam, and a threat to secularism in Quebec schools. Some voiced the opinion that newcomers should check their identity at the border, forgetting the behaviour of their own ancestors towards aboriginal communities, not to mention the Charter of Rights. At one point, a few schools requested able-bodied Muslim students not to observe the fast of Ramadan.

While the Quebec Human Rights Commission ruled that discrimination against the hijab was contrary to the provincial charter, it did not stop the province's largest teachers union from calling for a ban on the wearing of skullcaps, hijabs, and turbans in Quebec's public schools in 1995. While the vote was not enforced, militant secular voices remain strong in the province's education system.

Since then, the QHRC has helped to resolve more incidents of schools demanding that Muslim schoolgirls choose between their education and their hijab. Their recurrence indicates that tensions continue to exist. Given the developments in *la Republique Française*, there will be renewed calls in *la belle province* to ban all religious symbols, using the same arguments. Those who believe in building bridges of mutual respect, accommodation, and understanding will have to step forward.

A few years ago, I attended a lecture where a man complained to an Islamic scholar about discrimination:

"They kick our girls out from school. They do not hire women with hijabs. They do not respect our beliefs. What should we do?" The scholar, a Canadian convert, answered, "No one said this faith would be easy. You have to fight for what you believe in, within the system. This country has rules and laws that permit you to observe your faith. You have to work hard to educate people. Don't expect everything to be handed to you so easily. This test is part of your faith."

No Veiled Threat

Some time ago now, I stopped at a local mosque to offer my sunset prayers before heading off to a restaurant for an iftar dinner with friends. (Iftar is the meal that breaks the daylong fast during the month of Ramadan.) I met a pleasant young woman, who had removed her niqab (face veil) in the privacy of the women's section. She was gracious to all, offering dates and milk to break the fast. Her demeanour exuded a generous spirituality. While we spoke, she gently exhorted her children to stop running, restraining her exasperation when they disobeyed. What mother hasn't gone through this experience?

At the restaurant, a niqabi woman came up to me whom I did not recognize at first. Her eyes glistened with familiarity. "Assalaamu alaikum, Sheema. I see you more often on TV than in person," she joked. I immediately recognized her voice. We had first met fifteen years ago and had struck an instant friendship. Life had taken us in different directions; now we were both married with kids. She had memorized the entire Koran during that time, and was now teaching women and children to do the same.

I respect women who wear the niqab. At Harvard, after

much spiritual reflection, I donned the hijab (headscarf) and also tried the niqab—for all of one hour. I found it stifling and unnatural. Yet others don't. And their choice should be respected. In some places, women are forced by the state to cover up. In other places, some have exercised their own choice to do so. At a recent scientific conference in Dubai, I met intelligent, assertive niqabis who discussed current research with both genders. What is the big deal?

The niqab has been in the news recently, often in the most unflattering terms. These new WMDs (women in Muslim dress) seem to evoke the same fear once reserved for the other WMDs (weapons of mass destruction). The most vocal critics are European men in positions of power along with feminists. Few have taken the time to understand the issue from the point of view of the veiled women themselves.

The debate is eerily similar to the discourse that took place during the British occupation of Egypt in the late 1800s. Intent on controlling the natives, the Empire sought to weaken nationalist sentiment by stripping away indigenous Egyptian identity. In the colonial hierarchy, Victorian England was the pinnacle of civilization; the rest had to be civilized.

Lord Cromer (Evelyn Baring), the first British proconsul of Egypt, viewed Islam as the "other"—a faith utterly devoid of any good. In particular, he focused on the dress (i.e. the veil) and seclusion of Muslim women as emblematic of their oppression and inferiority. They were in need of rescue—by the Empire. He pushed the feminist envelope to ostensibly liberate Egyptian women. Yet during his rule, he greatly reduced women's access to education. When he returned to England, he opposed the women's movement at every turn. Feminism was good for the colonized, but not for the colonizer.

Many members of the Egyptian elite internalized the superiority of British civilization and championed Lord Cromer's call. One such person was Qasim Amin, who published the controversial tract *Liberation of Women* in 1899. In it, he derided all of Egyptian society for its inferiority. Women were described in the most misogynistic terms. In contrast, the sycophantic Amin extolled the virtues of the European male.

Amin was not interested in substantive issues of equality, such as women's education, health, or employment. His main focus was on the veil as the symbol of all of society's ills. It represented backwardness. He called on women to discard it so that Egypt could join the ranks of the civilized. He had as much interest in the welfare of Egyptian women as did Lord Cromer.

The reaction was predictable. An uproar ensued, with the greatest outrage expressed by nationalists. While many of them were not particularly religious, they championed the veil in reaction to colonialist designs.

Thus began a series of chain reactions, wherein the veil became a symbol, acquiring new meanings that were never part of classical Islamic teachings. It was a banner of resistance in Algeria (against the French) and Iran (against the Shah), a response to autocratic rulers who banned the veil as a symbol of inferiority. These simplistic debates deflected attention away from examination of substantive issues. Complex problems could simply be solved by either donning or discarding the veil.

Which brings us to recent events. In a Monty Pythonesque scenario, the British political establishment demanded that a particular minority (Muslims) integrate into British society, by coercing a minority within that minority to change its appearance. The British government had appropriated the veil as a symbol of "separateness" and an impediment to integration. In the 1890s, it symbolized backwardness and an impediment to civilization.

Integration is a complex issue. It is disingenuous to think

that discarding the niqab will engender a new path toward integration—especially into a society as hierarchical as that of the British. In a recent study by the Home Office, Muslim students were found to be far more tolerant than their non-Muslim counterparts. By placing full onus on the Muslim community, the government has abdicated its responsibility in the integration impasse. It also has embarked on a dangerously divisive path.

Especially at a time when an increasing number of Muslims see the "war on terror" as a "war on Islam," it is critical that cooler heads (covered or not) prevail, so that issues can be discussed objectively and dispassionately.

Hijabs:
Don't Kick Up a Fuss

"Soccer moms 'R' us" is a good way to describe the recreational league I play in. We are women, over thirty years of age, who get together every week in friendly, competitive matches. I am the only hijabi in the league, but no one has ever raised the issue of my head scarf being a safety hazard (unless I secretly wear hoop earrings underneath). I can see the ball clearly, and the head scarf is not hanging loosely around my jersey. In fact, I don't think anyone notices it any more. I'm simply known as "Number 13," and I've managed to score in a number of games. I've also avoided pulling muscles or twisting my ankle—an added bonus at my age—and the hijab is no impediment.

I first played soccer in high school and loved it from the start. I have coached a few girls' teams and played both competitively and recreationally (and did a stint with a team called the "Dirty Sox"). I am also an accredited coach with the Canadian Soccer Association.

Soccer's a great sport—playing it requires skills in ball control, passing, kicking, and heading. It's an inexpensive way of staying fit. It encourages teamwork and is the most popular sport on Earth—loved by more people than baseball, basketball and hockey (which I also play) combined.

And so I shook my head in disbelief and disappointment when I heard about Asmahan Mansour, age eleven, who was barred from playing in a Quebec tournament for wearing her hijab. The referee ruled it a safety hazard.

Yet the refs in Asma's two other tournament games had no problems with her headgear. Neither has this ever been an issue in Ontario, where Asma plays regularly. Her team, along with five other Ontario teams, boycotted the remainder of the weekend tournament in support of Asma.

Quebec soccer officials cited FIFA, the soccer world's governing body, as the source for their ban. According to Brigitte Frot, executive director of the Quebec Soccer Federation, FIFA rules don't allow for any jewellery or headgear. But on FIFA's website, laws governing player's equipment state that "equipment such as headgear, facemasks, knee and arm protectors made of soft, lightweight, padded material are not considered to be dangerous and are therefore permitted." There are pictures of soccer players in action wearing bandanas, glasses, and headbands.

The brouhaha in Laval, Quebec, seems to be a replay of what happened in Australia. A referee refused to allow a young woman called Afifa Saad to play while wearing her hijab. Both her team and the opposition supported her, and the match was called off. The Victorian Soccer Federation said Ms Saad, age twenty-one, one of the state's most promising strikers, deserved an apology. The federation also formally adopted a new rule allowing Muslim women to wear hijab in the field.

VSF chief executive Damien Brown said that "the hijab has been deemed from the outset not to be dangerous and on that basis there is no issue whatsoever with people wearing it." Mr Brown even proposed the hijab policy for possible adoption by FIFA, saying "we're trying to set an example that will be applied across the world."

Aside from his progressive stand on the rules, Mr Brown captured the essential spirit of soccer, noting that "one of the real advantages of soccer over any other sport is, of course, its cultural diversity and its appeal across all boundaries." It is this spirit that has escaped Quebec soccer officials.

In the delightful comedy *Bend It Like Beckham*, plucky Jesminder Bhamra tries to satisfy her parents' traditions with her desire to play professional soccer. It's a metaphor of a dilemma faced by so many young people—how to maintain a multiplicity of identities while remaining true to oneself.

Too bad that Quebec soccer officials, unable to bend, have stood in the way of a Muslim girl and her soccer dreams. However, Asma and her teammates, coaches, and supporters, have been true to themselves by making sure that the principle of fair play speaks louder.

Our Right to Flash Some Veil

A few years ago, the Canadian Muslim Network held a dinner on Parliament Hill to honour the many people who had helped Maher Arar and Monia Mazigh advance the cause of human rights in a post 9/11 era. That evening, a scholarship was launched, in the name of these two people, for students studying human rights law at the University of Ottawa. MPs from all the parties spoke eloquently about the need to protect rights in a climate of fear. At one point, Bloc Québécois Leader Gilles Duceppe assured the many Muslims in the audience that they would always be welcome as valued members of Quebec society. His words were in direct response to the "cry of Hérouxville."[1]

Mr Duceppe's sentiments seemed sincere at the time. But, oh how times have changed in this province. Given the Islamophobia on display during the Bouchard-Taylor hearings,[2] Quebec's Muslims—who form 0.7 percent of the population—wonder how welcome they really are. No Quebec politician has publicly countered the ugly xenophobia; rather, some pandered to it. There has not even been a heartfelt call for tolerance and mutual respect.

Instead, Premier Jean Charest has seconded the call by the Quebec Council on the Status of Women to develop a hierarchy of human rights. The council wants to ban all conspicuous religious symbols worn by public servants. It is particularly irked by the hijab and niqab, and is essentially telling Muslim women, "We know what is best for you; you can't possibly wear that thing out of free will, and if you do, you are too oppressed to know any better." Call it feminism on testosterone. Imagine telling that to Monia Mazigh—who fearlessly challenged three national governments and their security agencies. If the council has its way, Ms Mazigh[3] can never run for public office in her hijab, nor teach at a public university.

For all the hand-wringing over the symbolism of the hijab, it is foremost a piece of cloth. For some, it is part of their faith's requirement of modesty. For others, it is an element of their cultural tradition. Many young Muslimahs wear it as a symbol of identity—or rebellion. And yes, there are women who are forced to wear it against their will. Feminism is supposed to empower women to make their own choices. Instead, the council has framed the road to freedom on its own terms: the secular way, or the highway.

This is nothing but fear. In the 1960s, men feared strong women. Today, it seems strong women are feared by women. Assertive Muslim women do pose a challenge to feminism. First, there is the embrace of religion, rather than its rejection, that makes many in the feminist establishment queasy. Then there is the covering up of one's body in public. It's not that the body is an object of shame—quite the opposite. Muslim women value their bodies, they simply don't believe in flashing skin.

The fear of Islam is revealed in calls to keep religion a private affair, locked away in our homes. In the past, we tried to hide what we feared and felt ashamed of—for example, physical disability, homosexuality, mental illness. Many were ostracized and suffered discrimination. We realized how wrong it was to deny individuals full participation in society simply because they were different. Now, there are those whose identity is defined primarily by their relationship to God. Dare we deny them full rights?

In these dangerous times, the forces of exclusion must be countered. Ignorance must be vanquished with knowledge, and fear doused by courage. Unfortunately, there is little political will to meet these challenges. No problem. Decent people can lead where politicians fear to tread. Just look at the twelve-year-old teammates of Asmahan Mansour, who forfeited their games at a Quebec soccer tournament in support of the right of Asmahan to follow her religious conscience by wearing a head scarf on the pitch. They are the future.

1. see note on p.44.

2. "A contentious series of public hearings on cultural differences and immigrant integration," [cbc.ca] headed by philosopher Charles Taylor and sociologist Gérard Bouchard.

3. see article "Facing New Identities" on p.106.

Don't Misread the Koran

I met "Leila" ten years ago. She was nineteen, maybe twenty. She had left family and friends to join her new husband in Montreal. The marriage had soured; she bore the brunt of his frustrations. When she became pregnant, he demanded an abortion. When she refused, he punched her in the abdomen. The violence grew worse after the child was born. Leila finally called the police when he stabbed her in the hand. She was ready to start a new life, with infant in tow, at a shelter for battered immigrant women. Despite her ordeal, she maintained a sparkle in her eyes and flashed an infectious smile.

Leila was trying to reconnect with her faith, Islam, and the Muslim community. All the more astounding, given that her husband had told her that Islam gave him the right to inflict violence on his wife. Yet Leila knew with implacable certainty that his actions were anathema to her faith. She could easily separate his actions from his perverse interpretations. I, on the other hand, had a harder time, having heard too many stories like Leila's.

I related these incidents to Ridwan Yusuf, a wonderful soft-spoken imam from Nigeria, who listened patiently to my tirade at the impotence of our community leaders to speak out against conjugal violence: "Wife-beaters are absolving themselves of responsibility by saying that Islam gives them the right to do this, when clearly it does not. Who is teaching this to them? Why are not the men in our community speaking out against it? We scream indignation at the oppression of Muslims by others, but we remain silent about oppression from within."

Clearly moved, he pledged to cooperate with community leaders to assist vulnerable women and children. Volunteers came forward to offer moral and financial support, ready to learn more about the roots, symptoms, and treatment of the social blight that cuts across all societies.

Ridwan Yusuf had the courage to address the issue head-on at the largest community gathering of the year, the Eid prayer. He systematically stripped away the mantle of Islamic legitimacy shielding the practice of violence against wives, and followed with exhortations to build marriages based on love, mercy, and respect.

Prophet Muhammad never once laid a finger on any of his wives, instead he denounced those who did and asserted that those best in character are those who are best to their wives.

In 2004, a Spanish court sentenced an imam for inciting violence against women. He had written a book, *Women in Islam*, that included advice for Muslim men on how to beat their wives. He argued in his defence that he was merely repeating the opinions of medieval scholars. Muslim experts however, had testified that the imam's approach misinterpreted both the spirit and letter of Islamic teaching. Many Muslim groups agreed with the court's ruling.

Such small steps forward are necessary to counter regressive forces, some of which apply narrow, hateful interpretations to the (Arabic) text of the Koran. Islamic scholarship demands a comprehensive examination of all Koranic verses, with Prophet Muhammad's interpretation serving as the sublime example. To read the Koranic sura, or chapter, on women as condoning the beating of one's wife is to see it through the lens of one's own prejudices and is but a feeble attempt to justify one's misbehaviour.

We cannot discount the influence of religious figures in shaping attitudes towards women: the Taliban practice of banning female education was supported by scholars of the region. And the practice in some countries of female genital mutilation, which predates Islam, is often defended by those who link it outrageously with the Koran. A 1995 documentary on the subject featured a Somali man declaring: "Of course we do it. It is in the Koran." Of course it is not! But false attribution is comforting to those who stubbornly cling to vile cultural practices.

Uprooting Age-old Customs from Within

Ingrained cultural mores—especially those pertaining to women—are often impervious to criticism from without. Yet, it often takes a heinous event, rooted in those very mores, to shake attitudes from within. These reverberations can then uproot age-old customs, leading to social change. Such was the case of Mukhtar Mai in Pakistan.

Syria is now beginning to face the dishonourable custom of "honour killing," following the tragic case of sixteen-year-old Zahra al-Azzo. At the age of fifteen, she was kidnapped from her village outside Damascus and raped. After the perpetrator was caught, Zahra was placed in a women's prison by authorities who feared her family would "restore" the family honour by killing her. Instead, Zahra's cousin, Fawaz, offered to marry her. Everything seemed fine, until her brother broke into their apartment one morning and stabbed her repeatedly as she slept. That evening, her family celebrated.

Usually, it is taboo to mention such a killing. Yet Zahra's case touched a public nerve. Lawyers, Islamic scholars, and government officials forged a public campaign to change laws and attitudes that protect honour crimes. Under Syrian law, an honour killing is not murder, and the man who commits it is not a murderer. The Grand Mufti of Syria condemned honour killing in unequivocal terms, reminding the public that the Koran does not differentiate between women and men in its moral laws and requires sexual chastity of both.

In Egypt, a thirteen-year-old girl recently bled to death while undergoing genital mutilation at a village clinic. The government immediately shut down the clinic and banned all medical practitioners from involvement in such activities. The villagers (men and women) reacted in anger, insisting on maintaining the practice in spite of the recent death. This set off an intense nationwide debate, leading to a powerful public campaign to stop female genital mutilation. As in Syria, women's groups, the government, and religious officials combined efforts to confront centuries-old attitudes. Female circumcision is a common practice among Egyptian Christians and Muslims. It is linked to the notion of female "purity." Without it, a woman may be considered "unmarriageable."

The Egyptian Ministry of Religious Affairs issued a booklet explaining why the practice was not called for in Islam; Egypt's Grand Mufti, Ali Gomaa, declared it haram, or prohibited by Islam; Egypt's highest religious official, Muhammad Sayyid Tantawi, called it harmful. A national hotline was set up to answer the public's questions about genital cutting.

After a century of trying to eradicate the practice, it seems the tide is turning. The biggest hurdle in the way of eradication has been the taboo against publicly discussing female genital mutilation.

There is a similar evolution under way in several West African countries, where Islamic scholars and health-care workers have worked in tandem to address the harmful consequences of this practice. Communities are now taking collective action to abandon the centuries-old tradition.

Nearly 2,000 villages in Senegal have formally declared that cutting will no longer be allowed.

These tectonic shifts in attitude elsewhere have implications in Canada, as well. Recently a Carleton University student who was sexually assaulted issued a clarification that, contrary to news reports, she had not been raped. Initial accounts described a brutal attack: an unknown assailant entered the lab where she was working, broke her jaw, knocked her unconscious, and then sexually assaulted her, leaving her hospitalized for days.

Thereafter, the student identified herself as Muslim and issued the clarification to save herself from the stigma of rape. In certain cultures, this can have an adverse effect on marriage prospects. While few in the Muslim community know the woman's identity, some rightfully asked: why should a victim of sexual assault carry any guilt about rape? This woman needs support and comfort from her community, not stigmatization. National and local Muslim organizations issued statements in support of her, and condemned the stigma of rape.

For once, this taboo subject has been broached from within. But where are the imams and religious leaders? As in Syria, Egypt, and Senegal, their voices are essential for changing disturbing cultural attitudes towards rape and abuse. After all, Prophet Muhammad punished those who molested women, without ever stigmatizing the victims.

The Koran Does Not Sanction
Wife-beating

Public focus on domestic violence is relatively new. In 1982, a chorus of laughter in the House of Commons greeted NDP MP Margaret Mitchell's mention of a report on wife-beating. On occasion, our judges have made insensitive remarks about violence against women. In 1989, Quebec Court Judge Denys Dionne observed during a trial that "rules are like a woman, they are made to be violated."

Today, such comments would be met with wide public outrage. Zero tolerance means that there is no plausible excuse for allowing a man to beat his wife or partner. Many nations also have come to abide by this principle.

Such was not the case in Germany when Judge Christa Datz-Winter cited the Koran in turning down a German Muslim woman's request for a speedy divorce on the ground that her husband beat her. The judge noted that the couple were of Moroccan culture, in which "it is not unusual that the husband uses physical punishment against the wife." The Koran, she wrote in her decision, sanctions such physical abuse.

The ruling was condemned by all segments of German society, including the Muslim community. Everyone agreed that German law should supersede any cultural or religious context. Muslim leaders were also offended by the judge's interpretation of the Koran. Her clumsy attempt at multicultural understanding turned out to be a serious judicial misstep. For this, she was removed from the case.

Interestingly, neither culture nor the Koran was cited by the defence.

In Ottawa, a similar court case—with an important twist—was reaching its conclusion at about the same time.

A man was convicted of assaulting his wife four times and threatening to kill her. He was a PhD candidate; she was a master's student in engineering. The beatings began the day after she gave birth, and continued for more than a year. Despite the abuse, she kept returning to her husband—which is not that uncommon in such cases. She was new to the country, had no family here, and her husband controlled her finances. She feared that the Children's Aid Society would take the children if she went to the police, and that she would be deported.

The twist? The woman testified that the Koran gave a husband permission to beat his wife. In addition, the judge wrote that the husband "may have believed that it was his right to beat his wife." And while the judge had to consider "religious and cultural norms," she made it clear that "the law applies to all residents."

There needs to be an honest examination of the Koranic passage—Chapter 4, Verse 34—that supposedly sanctions wife-beating. The verb in question, "dharaba," is invariably translated as "to beat," even though it also means "to leave." The Prophet Muhammad—who is the example for all Muslims to follow—never struck any of his wives. He admonished those who did.

Yet, many translations and classical Koranic commentaries counsel striking one's wife. Mawlana Mawdudi, an influential figure from South Asia, wrote that some women were actually in need of a beating. Some scholars temper this approach by saying that the beating should be administered with something as "light" as a twig. With so many religious authorities advocating beating in one form or another, is it any surprise that Muslim men—and women—find it acceptable?

Thankfully, there are exceptions. During a recent Friday sermon, Imam Abdurrahman Alhejazy of Ottawa spoke forcefully against domestic abuse, reminding congregants of the Prophet's example. Egypt's Grand Mufti, Sheik Ali Gomaa, has said, "Hitting one's wife is totally inappropriate." More voices are speaking out.

Not everyone agrees with this approach. Last year, the Canadian office of the Islamic Society of North America (ISNA) threatened to ban a new English translation of the Koran that advocated a man "leave," rather than "beat," his wife. The threat was overruled by Ingrid Mattson, the Canadian-born president of the ISNA.

There is this question for Muslims to consider: are women inferior, or worthy of the same treatment as men?

A Hero for Our Times

"I want to kill illiteracy."

Of all the statements on her website, the one above speaks to the strength of tremendous character of Mukhtar Mai Bibi.

Ms Mai is not your average literacy crusader. In June, 2002, Ms Mai was gang-raped on the order of a rural Pakistani tribal council as "compensation" for an alleged slight of tribal honour. With the council's approval, she was dragged away to a hut and sexually assaulted by four men. Her father was held at gunpoint during the ordeal. The poor woman was left to walk home half-clothed before a crowd of onlookers. Following this brutality, her family was intimidated, so that they were unwilling to file a police report.

The incident would have remained hidden, had it not been for the courage of Abdul Razzaq, a local imam who condemned the act during a sermon, at great risk to his life, saying, "Such a barbaric and oppressive injustice has never been witnessed before." Local media picked up the imam's comments.

The attack galvanized people to demand zero tolerance of tribal law by the government, which replied uncharacteristically swiftly. Eighteen men were arrested; some of the rapists were put on death row.

As a deterrent to such violence, the government widely publicized the case. It sent armed guards to protect Ms Mai and her family, offered more than $8,000 (US) as compensation and promised to provide electricity, paved roads, and a police outpost for the village. As well, it promised to build schools—one each for boys and girls—and to name the girls' school for Ms Mai. Here she would also be able to study. Rather than ostracize the victim of a brutal rape, the government put the onus of shame where it belongs—on the rapists and the council.

Initially, Ms Mai thought of committing suicide—the "traditional" route taken by many rural women who are raped. Why? In such a toxic cultural environment, it is the assaulted woman who has lost all honour in the eyes of the village, and is seen as a source of shame for her family. Where honour killing is prevalent, such misogynist views are held by both men and women.

Instead, empowered by her faith, she testified against her attackers. Refusing to wallow in victimhood, she used the compensation money to contribute to the school in her firm belief that education is the way to change attitudes. But while Ms Mai has remained true to her cause, the government's commitment has waned. *The New York Times* reported that the school may have to close due to lack of funds for operating expenses. Ms Mai has had to pay some school expenses, and to provide food for the police who protect her. Meanwhile, villagers were waiting to take vengeance on Ms Mai and her family once the police left.

Despite all the obstacles, Mukhtar Mai Bibi strives to improve the lives of those around her. She no longer relies on government handouts. With the help of a former law student, she has formed a welfare organization whose goal is to improve the health, literacy, and economic independence of rural women. She is also seeking an end to brutal tribal practices. Education will have a key role, and she plans to open more schools in rural areas.

After her story ran in the *Times*, a supporter in the US helped set up a website devoted to her cause: http://www.mukhtarmai.com. This is all the more astounding, given that her village still lacks its promised electricity.

The website is inspiring for its simplicity, sincerity and ambition. Mukhtar Mai Bibi's goal is simple: to make "today's woman stronger" in a culture where submissiveness is the norm. Her next step is more mundane: to ensure that donations of money and books by supporters navigate through the labyrinth of government bureaucracy and arrive at their proper destination.

Through her example and determination, Ms Mai has inspired countless other women and men to strive against injustice. But perhaps more important, she has a clear vision for the future in her desire to improve educational opportunities for young girls.

What Closed-minded Liberals
Can Learn from a Rape Victim

'You've been brainwashed!" asserted my good friend Nazila. (I've changed her name.) We were in the final stages of graduate school at Harvard, she in fine arts, I in chemical physics. Nazila was staunchly secular, having fled the Iranian revolution with her family for the safe haven of America. I had been nominally Muslim until late 1988, when I went through a spiritual reawakening after much soul searching. The changes inside me were partly reflected in changes outside, consisting of a greater modesty in appearance and behaviour. My hijab threw most people for a loop.

Like Nazila, many of the über-liberals at Harvard insisted that these changes in me were due to my utter lack of personal choice in the matter: I must have been brainwashed by religion. Of course, before I "got religion," my friends thought my mind was perfectly fine. Many of these same intellectuals decided on the demarcation point of my brainwashing: when I no longer subscribed to a view devoid of spiritual purpose.

I realized that those who professed to be liberal and progressive did so on the following premise: "Of course we are open-minded, so long as your world view agrees with ours."

This is a theme that is applied often, if not always, to Muslim women who choose to abide by the teachings of their faith. We are seen as poor ill-informed souls who cannot think for ourselves. For if we did, how could we choose such a path? Consider the condescending tone of the recent sharia debate. Detractors of faith-based arbitration would always trot out the immigrant Muslim woman who spoke little English (or French) as a raison d'être for an arbitration ban.

She needed to be rescued since she was assumed to be so helpless, so infantile that she could not make a choice for herself. The irony is that such wholesale character assassinations are used by many a misogynistic Muslim commentator.

And yet, a barely literate, rural Pakistani woman, with no English skills whatsoever, received *Glamour* magazine's Woman of the Year Award in New York. Mukhtar Mai responded to a brutal gang rape (ordered by a village tribal council) with a campaign of education for the children of her village in Pakistan. In a recent interview, Anna Maria Tremonti of CBC Radio's *The Current* asked Ms Mai about the source of her courage. She replied that it came first from God, and then from her family. When asked about her generosity toward the village, Ms Mai observed that it was "a matter of choice" to spread the wealth of financial compensation for the benefit of many. Faith and choice are the core values of Ms Mai—and that of many Muslim women worldwide.

What many neosecularists cannot grasp is the desire to cultivate a deep personal connection with God in daily life. Some declare an absolute separation of church and state. Yet Canada's very Charter asserts, "Whereas Canada is founded upon principles that recognize the supremacy of God and the rule of law. . ." As Svend Robinson discovered a few years ago, Canadians overwhelmingly oppose removing the reference to God in the highest law of the land. It is not merely a preamble.

Our modern world offers very little solace to the spirit. It assaults the senses with materialism and fear. Individuals seek their own way to cope with these. For some, strength is derived from faith. For many Muslim women, that has meant self-inquiry and searching for their place in the grand scheme of things—and finding that peace from the teachings of the Koran. It is a noble endeavour, a personal journey that requires thought and choice. It may mean making choices that differ from Western feminist paradigms. All fair in the marketplace of ideas. Yet some, whose ideas are soundly rejected, find fault with the discerning buyer, rather than the unsuitability of their one-size-fits-all ideology.

To those who insist that our choice is misguided, dangerous, or perhaps brain-wasting: To you your way, to me mine. Many of us have experienced a purely secular outlook and found it to be thoroughly unsatisfying, for it fails to address the dynamic of one's spiritual core. That inner voice, hidden to all except to the One who created it and who alone can respond to it.

And so we carry on, expecting the taunts and attacks on our choices. These only strengthen our resolve to be true to ourselves, as women who find purpose in faith. Moral choices made by Muslim women: a novel concept? Perhaps for casual observers who assume so much and know so little. Not so those who live the faith day in and day out, like Mukhtar Mai.

The Sorrow and the Pity of "Honour"

In pre-Islamic Arabia, the concept of male honour was so inflated, that the birth of a female child was often seen as a source of shame. Female infanticide was not uncommon. Historical records describe a man who took his daughter out to the desert to bury her. As he dug her grave, the innocent child tried to shield him from the dust and brushed it away from his beard.

Unmoved, he buried her alive.

This heinous practice was directly addressed during the twenty-three-year period of Koranic revelation. First, negative attitudes towards the birth of girls were strongly condemned. The Koran warned that the buried daughter would be raised one day to testify against her murderer. The Prophet Muhammad advocated for the benevolent treatment of children, putting special emphasis on fair treatment of daughters. Many who had either supported or committed female infanticide were moved to remorse. Laws were passed against infanticide. In just over two decades, this barbaric tradition was outlawed by the very tribes that had previously embraced it as part of male honour.

Muslims proudly point to the above example of the establishment of social justice through Islamic principles. Yet we seem to forget that this example is not merely a showpiece of the past, but a blueprint for addressing injustices of the present.

In December 2005, after attending the congregational Friday prayer in East Punjab, Nazir Ahmed bought a butcher's knife and methodically slit the throats of his twenty-five-year-old stepdaughter and his three daughters, of ages eight, seven and four. He suspected the stepdaughter of adultery, an act he considered tantamount to treason. In order to restore his "lost honour," he killed her, and then killed his own daughters for good measure to ensure that they wouldn't follow in her footsteps. When apprehended, he expressed satisfaction that he had preserved his "honour."

"Honour killing" is the mother of all oxymorons. According to the Human Rights Commission of Pakistan, 260 cases of honour killings were recorded in 2005. Such murderous acts also occur in Turkey and the Middle East and have been reported within immigrant communities in Europe.

Let's be clear: such a custom is unequivocally condemned by Islam.

Muslims have reacted in various ways to this phenomenon. Many of them, of course, distance themselves from this evil. A few courageous activists have campaigned actively to eradicate this evil. On the other hand, conspiracy-seekers point to news accounts of honour killings as another example of anti-Muslim media bias—showing more concern with negative PR than with the ugly reality plaguing certain Muslim cultures.

We Muslims have a greater responsibility than the mere preservation of image. We have a duty to address social injustice head on, following the footsteps of our prime example, Prophet Muhammad. As individuals, we must speak out against this barbaric practice, using the very principles of our faith. Those who support this custom falsely claim legitimacy from Islam. We can no longer disagree politely; we must confront such immorality and strip away all claims of legitimacy.

Religious principles can be used as part of a comprehensive approach to change deep-rooted misogynistic customs. This is happening today in parts of Africa, where societies are confronting another age-old barbarism: female genital mutilation. Womankind Kenya, a grassroots group opposed to FGM, tried unsuccessfully for years to convince female "cutters" to abandon their trade. Then it joined forces with respected local imams, arranging for them to travel to villages and speak with women (and men) about the evil of such a practice, which has no sanction in the Koran. People were told that the vagina was a part of the body, created by God, and as important as a limb or an eye. Cutting it was a sin, for which one would be held accountable before God.

The appeal to the conscience of Muslims has had resounding effects. Many have laid down their knives, asked for forgiveness from their victims, and have become anti-FGM advocates. The practice is losing favour; African governments have outlawed the custom. Slowly, the tide seems to be turning.

The model adopted by Womankind Kenya should be used to combat "honour killings" in Muslim cultures. While there are no reports of such killings in Canada, we must remain vigilant.

Following the July 7 bombings in London, imams across Canada demonstrated moral leadership by issuing a statement condemning extremism in all its forms. They used their religious authority to make it abundantly clear that there is no room for hateful, murderous attitudes in our Canadian communities. Many of these same imams have also spoken against the ill-treatment of women. They can contribute towards the eradication of honour killing by addressing this issue during sermons where large congregations of Muslims gather.

Attempts to change oppressive cultural traditions will meet with resistance. All the more reason to increase our resolve to replace oppression with justice, cruelty with compassion.

Acknowledgements

Patrick Martin and (the late) Val Ross of *The Globe and Mail* were instrumental in providing a unique writing opportunity; their moral support, mentorship and patience are sincerely appreciated.

The generous encouragement of the following individuals, cannot go unmentioned: Natasha Hassan, Edward Greenspon and the *Globe* editorial team; Michael Adams, Hadeel Al-Shalchi, Nancy Avery, Natasha Bakht, Rhonda Birenbaum, Alan Borovoy, Jonathan Cohen, Penny Collenette, Ibrahim Danial, Bronwyn Drainie, Catherine Eckenswiller, Amira Elghawaby, Omaima Faris, Ihsaan Gardee, Steve Garland, Wael Haddara, Khadija Haffajee, Rubina Hussain, Abdul-Basit Khan, Meena Khan, Sheeba Khan, Faisal Kutty, Daphne Lainson, Sufia Lodhi, Roy MacGregor, Monia Mazigh, Neil Milton, Joy Morrow, Al O'Brien, John Ohnjec, Francine Pelletier, Kerry Pither, Anna Porter, Naeem and Riad Saloojee, Mariam Sheibani and Leslie Seidle.

This project could not have been possible without the commitment of TSAR Publications, and in particular, Nurjehan Aziz. Her cheerful, sanguine approach has made this first book project an enjoyable venture.

I wish to also thank my husband Tareq, and our children Sara, Ziyad and Dalia for their unyielding love and patience. Finally, a special thanks to my parents, Shamim and Shoaib Khan, who raised us with understanding, compassion, and love for the simplicities of life —all the while harmonizing the spirit of Islam with the best of Canadian values.